MISS
MCDONALD

MRS. MARY J. HOLMES

Miss McDonald

Mary J. Holmes

© 1st World Library, 2007
PO Box 2211
Fairfield, IA 52556
www.1stworldlibrary.com
First Edition

LCCN: 2007934199

Softcover ISBN: 978-1-4218-9662-5
Hardcover ISBN: 978-1-4218-9762-2
eBook ISBN: 978-1-4218-9562-8

Purchase *"Miss McDonald"*
as a traditional bound book at:
www.1stWorldLibrary.com/purchase.asp?ISBN=978-1-4218-9662-5

1st World Library is a literary, educational organization
dedicated to:

- Creating a free internet library of downloadable ebooks

- Hosting writing competitions and offering book publishing
scholarships.

Interested in more 1st World Library books? contact:
literacy@1stworldlibrary.com
Check us out at: www.1stworldlibrary.com

1ˢᵗ World Library Literary Society

Giving Back to the World

"If you want to work on the core problem, it's early school literacy."

- James Barksdale, former CEO of Netscape

"No skill is more crucial to the future of a child, or to a democratic and prosperous society, than literacy."

- Los Angeles Times

"Literacy... means far more than learning how to read and write... The aim is to transmit... knowledge and promote social participation."

- UNESCO

"Literacy is not a luxury, it is a right and a responsibility. If our world is to meet the challenges of the twenty-first century we must harness the energy and creativity of all our citizens."

- President Bill Clinton

"Parents should be encouraged to read to their children, and teachers should be equipped with all available techniques for teaching literacy, so the varying needs and capacities of individual kids can be taken into account."

- Hugh Mackay

CONTENTS

CHAPTER I

EXTRACTS FROM MISS FRANCES THORNTON'S JOURNAL

ELMWOOD, June 15, 18—

I have been out among my flowers all the morning, digging, weeding, and transplanting, and then stopping a little to rest. Such perfect successes as my roses are this year, while my white lilies are the wonder of the town, and yet my heart was not with them to-day, and it was nothing to me that those fine people staying at the Towers came into the grounds while I was at work, "just to see and admire," they said, adding that there was no place like Elmwood in all the town of Cuylerville. I know that, and Guy and I have been so happy here, and I loved him so much, and never dreamed what was in store for me until it came so suddenly and seemed like a heavy blow.

Why did he want to get married, when he has lived to be thirty years old, without a care of any kind, and with money enough to allow him to indulge his taste for books, and pictures, and travel, and is respected by everybody, looked up to as the first man in town, and petted and cared for by me as few brothers have ever been petted and cared for; why, I say, did he want a change, and, if he must be married, why need he take a child of sixteen, whom he has only known since Christmas, and whose sole recommendation, so far as I can learn, is her pretty face?

Daisy McDonald is her name, and she lives in Indianapolis, where her father is a poor lawyer, and Guy met her last winter in Chicago and fell in love at once, and made two or three journeys West on "important business," he said, and then, some time in May, told me he was going to bring me a sister, the sweetest little creature, with such beautiful blue eyes and wonderful hair. I was sure to love her, he said, and when I suggested that she was very young, he replied that her youth was in her favor, as he could more easily mold her to the Thornton pattern.

Little he knows about girls, but then he was perfectly infatuated and blind to everything but Daisy's eyes, and hair, and voice, which is so sweet and winning that it will *speak* for her at once; and he asked me to see to the furnishing of the rooms on the west side of the house, two which communicate with his own private library, where he spends a great deal of time with his books and writing. The room adjoining this he would have for Daisy's boudoir or parlor, where she could sit when he was occupied and she wished to be near him. This he would have fitted up in blue, as she had expressed a wish to that effect, and he said no expense must be spared to make it as pretty and attractive as possible. So the walls were frescoed and tinted, and I spent two entire days in New York hunting for a carpet of the desirable shade, which should be right both in texture and design.

Guy was exceedingly particular, and developed a wonderful proclivity to find fault with everything I admired. Nothing was quite the thing for Daisy until at last a manufacturer offered to get one up which should suit, and so the carpet question was happily ended for the time being. Then came the furniture, and unlimited orders were given to the upholsterer to do his best, and matters were progressing finely when order number two came from the little lady, who was sorry to seem so fickle, but mamma, whose taste was perfect, had decided against all blue, and would Guy please furnish the room with drab trimmed with blue. "It must be a very delicate shade of drab," she wrote, and lest he should get too intense an idea, she would call it a *tint* of a *shade* of drab, or, better yet, a *hint* of a tint of a shade of drab would describe exactly what she meant, and be so entirely unique, and lovely, and recherche.

Guy never swears, and seldom uses slang of any kind, but this was a little too much, and with a most rueful expression of countenance he asked me "what in thunder I supposed a hint of a tint of a shade of drab could be."

I could not enlighten him, and we finally concluded to leave it to the upholsterer, to whom Guy telegraphed in hot haste, bidding him hunt New York over for the desired shade. Where he found it I never knew, but find it he did, or something approximating to it, a faded, washed-out color, which seemed a cross between wood-ashes and pale skim milk. A sample was sent up for Guy's approval, and then the work commenced again, when order number three came in one of those dainty little billets which used to make Guy's face radiant with happiness. Daisy had changed her mind again and gone back to the blue, which she always preferred as most becoming to her complexion.

Guy did not say a single word, but he took the next train for New York and stayed there till the furniture was done and packed for Cuylerville. As I did not know where he was stopping, I could not forward him two little missives which came during his absence, and which bore the Indianapolis post-mark. I suspect he had a design in keeping his hotel from me, and whether Daisy changed her mind again or not I never knew.

The furniture reached Elmwood the day but one before Guy started for his bride, and Julia Hamilton, who was then at the Towers, helped me arrange the room, which is a perfect little gem and cannot fail to please, I am sure. I wonder Guy never fancied Julia Hamilton. Oh, if he only had done so I should not have as many misgivings as I now have nor dread the future so much. Julia is sensible and twenty years old, and lives in Boston, and comes of a good family, and is every way suitable; but when did a man ever choose the woman whom his sister thought suitable for him? And Guy is like other men, and this is his wedding day; and after a trip to Montreal, and Quebec, and Boston, and New York, and Saratoga, they are coming home, and I am to give a grand reception and then subside, I suppose, into the position of the "old maid sister who will be dreadfully in the way."

SEPTEMBER 15, 18—

Just three months since I opened my Journal, and, on glancing over what I wrote on Guy's wedding day, I find that in one respect at least I was unjust to the little creature who is now my sister and calls me Miss Frances. Not by a word or look has she shown the least inclination to assume the position of mistress of the house, nor does she seem to think me at all in the way; but that she considers me quite an antediluvian I am certain, for, in speaking of something which happened in 1820, she asked if I remembered it! And I only three years older than Guy! But then she once called him a dear old grandfatherly man, and thought it a good joke that on their wedding tour she was mistaken for his daughter. She looks so young—not sixteen even; but with those childish blue eyes, and that innocent, pleading kind of expression, she never can be old. She is very beautiful, and I can understand in part Guy's infatuation, though at times he hardly knows what to do with his pretty plaything.

It was the middle of August when they came from Saratoga, sorely against her wishes, as I heard from the Porters, who were at the same hotel, and who have told me what a sensation she created, and how much attention she received. Everybody flattered her, and one evening when there was to be a hop at Congress Hall, she received twenty bouquets from as many different admirers, each of whom asked her hand for the first dance. They had ascertained that Guy was not a disciple of Terpsichore, though I understand he did try some of the square dances, with poor success, I imagine, for Lucy Porter laughed when she told me of it; and I do not wonder, for my grave, scholarly Guy must be as much out of place in a ball room as his little, airy doll of a wife is in her place when there. I can understand just how she enjoyed it all, and how she hated to come home, for she did not then know the kind of home she was coming to.

It was glorious weather for August, and a rain of the previous day had washed all the flowers and shrubs, and freshened up the grass on the lawn, which was just like a piece of velvet, while everything around Elmwood seemed to laugh in the warm afternoon sunshine as the carriage came up to the door. Eight trunks, two hat-boxes, and a guitar-case had come in the morning, and were waiting the arrival of their owner, whose face looked eagerly out at the house and its surroundings, and, it seemed to me, did not light up as much as it should have done under the circumstances.

"Why, Guy, I always thought the house was brick," I heard her say as the carriage door was opened by the coachman.

"No, darling—wood. Ah, there's Fan," was Guy's reply, and the next moment I had her in my arms.

Yes, literally in my arms. She is such a wee little thing, and her face is so sweet, and her eyes so childish and wistful, and her voice so musical and flute-like that before I knew what I was doing I lifted her from her feet and hugged her hard and said I meant to love her, first for Guy's sake and then for her own. Was it my fancy, I wonder, or did she really shrink back a little and put up her hands to arrange the bows and streamers and curls floating away from her like the flags on a vessel on some gala day?

She was very tired, Guy said, and ought to lie down before dinner. Would I show her to her room with Zillah, her maid? Then for the first time I noticed a dark-haired girl who had alighted from the carriage and stood holding Daisy's traveling bag and wraps.

"Her waiting maid, whom we found in Boston," Guy explained when we were alone. "She is so young and helpless, and wanted one so badly, that I concluded to humor her for a time, especially as I had not the most remote idea how to pin on those wonderful fixings which she wears. It is astonishing how many things it takes to make up the *tout ensemble* of a fashionable woman," Guy said, and I thought he glanced a little curiously at my plain cambric wrapper and smooth hair.

Indeed he has taken it upon himself to criticise me somewhat! thinks I am too slim, as he expresses it, and that my head might be improved if it had a more snarly appearance. Daisy, of course, stands for his model, and her hair does not look as if it had been combed in a month, and yet Zillah spends hours over it. She—that is, Daisy—was pleased with her boudoir, and gave vent to sundry exclamations of delight when she entered it and skipped around like the child she is, and said she was so glad it was blue instead of that indescribable drab, and that room is almost the only thing she has expressed an opinion about since she has been here. She does not talk much except to Zillah, and then in French, which I do not understand. If I were to write just what I think I should say that she had expected a great deal more grandeur than she finds. At all events, she takes the things which I think very nice and even elegant as a matter of course, and if we were to set up a style of living equal to that of the Queen's household I do believe she would act as if she had been accustomed to it all her life; or, at least, that it was what she had a right to expect. I know she imagines Guy a great deal richer than he is; and that reminds me of something which troubles me.

Guy has given his name to Dick Trevylian for one hundred thousand dollars. To be sure, it is only for three months, and Dick is worth three times that amount, and an old friend and every way reliable and honest. And still I did not want Guy to sign. I wonder why it is that women will always jump at a conclusion without any apparent reason. Of course, I could not explain it, but when Guy told me what he was going to do, I felt in an instant as if he would have it all to pay and told him so, but he only laughed at me and called me nervous and fidgety, and said a friend was good for nothing if he could not lend a helping hand occasionally. Perhaps that is true, but I was uneasy, and shall be glad when the time is up and the paper canceled.

Our expenses since Daisy came are double what they were before, and if we were to lose one hundred thousand dollars now we should be badly off. Daisy is a luxury Guy has to pay for, but he pays willingly and seems to grow more and more infatuated every day. "She is such a sweet-tempered, affectionate little puss," he says; and I admit to myself that she is sweet-tempered, and that nothing ruffles her, but about the affectionate part I am not so certain. Guy would pet her and caress her all the time if she would let him, but she won't.

"Oh, please don't touch me. It is too warm, and you muss my dress," I have heard her say more than once when he came in and tried to put his arm about her or take her in his lap.

Indeed, her dress seems to be uppermost in her mind, and I have known her to try on half a dozen different ones before she could decide in which she looked the best. No matter what Guy is doing, or how deeply he is absorbed in his studies, she makes him stop and inspect her from all points and give his opinion, and Guy submits in a way perfectly wonderful to me who never dared to disturb him when shut up with his books.

Another thing, too, he submits to which astonishes me more than anything else. It used to annoy him terribly to wait for anything or anybody. He was always ready, and expected others to be, but Daisy is just the reverse. Such dawdling habits I never saw in any person. With Zillah to help her dress she is never ready for breakfast, never ready for dinner, never ready for church, never ready for anything, and that, in a household accustomed to order and regularity, does put things back so and make so much trouble.

"Don't wait breakfast for me, please," she says, when she has been called for the third or fourth time, and if she can get us to sit down without her she seems to think it all right, and that she can dawdle as much as she likes.

I wonder that it never occurs to her that to keep the breakfast table round, as we must, makes the girls cross and upsets the kitchen generally. I hinted as much to her once when the table stood till ten o'clock, and she only opened her great blue eyes wonderingly, and said mamma had spoiled her, but she would try and do better, and she bade Zillah call her at

Mary J. Holmes

five the next morning, and Zillah called her, and then she was a half-hour late. Guy doesn't like that, and he looked daggers on the night of the reception, when the guests began to arrive before she was dressed! And she commenced her toilet, too, at three o'clock! But she was wondrously beautiful in her bridal robes, and took all hearts by storm. She is perfectly at home in society, and knows just what to do and say so long as the conversation keeps in the fashionable round of chit-chat, but when it drifts into deeper channels she is silent at once, or only answers in monosyllables. I believe she is a good French scholar, and she plays and sings tolerably well, and reads the novels as they come out, but of books and literature, in general, she is wholly ignorant, and if Guy thought to find in her any sympathy with his favorite studies and authors he is terribly mistaken.

And yet, as I write all this, my conscience gives me sundry little pricks as if I were wronging her, for in spite of her faults I like her, and like to watch her flitting through the house and grounds like the little fairy she is, and I hope the marriage may turn out well, and that she will improve with age, and not make so heavy drafts on my brother's purse.

CHAPTER II

EXTRACTS FROM GUY'S JOURNAL

SEPTEMBER 20, 18—

Three months married. Three months with Daisy all to myself, and yet not exactly to myself either, for except I go after her I confess she does not often come to me, unless it is just as I have shut myself up in my room, thinking to have a quiet hour with my books. Then she generally appears, and wants me to ride with her, or play croquet, or see which dress is most becoming, and I always submit and obey her as if I were the child instead of herself.

She is young, and I almost wonder her mother allowed her to marry. Fan hints that they were mercenary, but if they were they concealed the fact wonderfully well, and made me think it a great sacrifice on their part to give me Daisy. And so it was; such a lovely little darling, and so beautiful. What a sensation she created at Saratoga, and still I was glad to get away, for I did not like some things which were done there. I did not like so many young men around her, nor her dancing those abominable round dances which she seemed to enjoy so much. "Square dances were poky," she said, even after I tried them with her for the sake of keeping her out of that vile John Britton's arms. I have a fancy that I made a

Mary J. Holmes

spectacle of myself, hopping about like a magpie, but Daisy said "I did beautifully," though she cried because I put my foot on her lace flounce and tore it, and I noticed she ever after had some good reason why I should not dance again. "It was too hard work for me; I was too big," she said, "and would tire easily. Cousin Tom was big, and he never danced."

By the way, I have some little curiosity with regard to that Cousin Tom who wanted Daisy so badly and who, because she refused him, went off to South America. I trust he will stay there. Not that I am or could be jealous of Daisy, but it is better for cousins like Tom to keep away.

Daisy is very happy here, though she is not quite so enthusiastic over the place as I supposed she would be, knowing how she lived at home. Well enough, it is true, and the McDonalds are intensely respectable, so she says; but her father's practice cannot bring him over two thousand a year, and the small brown house they live in, with only a grass plot in the rear and at the side, is not to be compared with Elmwood, which is a fine old place, everyone admits. It has come out gradually that she thought the house was brick and had a tower and billiard room, and that we kept more servants, and had a fishpond on the premises, and velvet carpets all over the house. I would not let Fan know this for the world, as I want her to like Daisy thoroughly.

And she does like her, though this little pink and white pet of mine is a new revelation to her, and puzzles her amazingly. She would have been glad if I had married Julia Hamilton of Boston; but those Boston girls are too strong-minded and positive to suit me. Julia is nice, it is true, and pretty and highly educated, and Fan says she has brains and would make a splendid wife. As Fan had never seen Daisy she did not, of course, mean to hint that she had not brains, but I suspect even now she would be better pleased if Julia were here, but I should not. Julia is self-reliant; Daisy is not. Julia has opinions of her own and asserts them, too; Daisy does not. Julia can sew and run a machine; Daisy cannot. Julia gets up in the morning and goes to bed at night; Daisy does neither. Nobody ever waits for Julia; everybody waits for Daisy. Julia reads scientific works and dotes on metaphysics; Daisy does not know the meaning of the word. In short, Julia is a strong, high-toned, energetic, independent woman, while Daisy is—a little innocent, confiding girl, whom I would rather have without brains than all the Boston women like Julia with brains!

And yet I sometimes wish she did care for books, and was more interested in what interests me. I have tried reading aloud to her an hour every evening, but she generally goes to sleep or steals up behind me to look over my shoulder and see how near I am to the end of the chapter, and when I reach it she says: "Excuse me, but I have just thought of something I must tell Zillah about the dress I want to wear to-morrow. I'll be back in a moment"; and off she goes, and our reading is ended for that time, for I notice she never returns. The dress is of more importance than the book, and I find her at ten or eleven trying to decide whether black or white or blue is most becoming to her. Poor Daisy! I fear she had no proper training at home. Indeed, she told me the other day that from her earliest recollection she had been taught that the main object of her life was to marry young and to marry money. Of course she did not mean anything or know how it sounded, but I would rather she had not said it, even though she had refused a millionaire for me, who can hardly be called rich as riches are rated these days. If Dick Trevylian should fail to meet his payment I should be very poor, and then what would become of Daisy, to whom the luxuries which money buys are so necessary?

(Here followed several other entries in the journal, consisting mostly of rhapsodies on Daisy, and then came the following:)

DECEMBER 15, 18—

Dick has failed to meet his payment, and that after having borrowed of me twenty thousand more! Is he a villain, and did he know all the time that I was ruining myself? I cannot think so when I remember that look on his face as he told me about it and swore to me solemnly that up to the very last he fully expected relief from England, where he thought he had a fortune.

"If I live I will pay you some time," he said; but that does not help me now. I am a ruined man. Elmwood must be sold, and I must work to earn my daily bread. For myself I would not mind it much, and Fan, who, woman-like, saw it in the distance and warned me of it, behaves nobly; but it falls hard on Daisy.

Poor Daisy! She never said a word when I told her the exact truth, but she went to bed and cried for one whole day. I am so glad I settled that ten thousand on her when we were married. No one can touch that, and I told her so; but she did not say a word or seem to know what I meant. Talking or expressing her opinion was never in her line, and she has not of her own accord spoken with me on the subject, and when I try to talk with her about our future she shudders and cries, and says, "Please don't! I can't bear it. I want to go home to mother!"

And so it was settled that while we are arranging matters she is to visit her mother and perhaps not return till spring, when I hope to be in a better condition financially than I am at present.

One thing Daisy said, which hurt me cruelly, and that was: "If I must marry poor, I might as well have married Cousin Tom, who wanted me so badly!" To do her justice, however, she added immediately: "But I like you the best."

I am glad she said that. It will be something to remember when she is gone, or rather when I return without her, as I am going to Indianapolis with her, and then back to the dreary business of seeing what I have left and what I can do. I have an offer for the house, and shall sell at once; but where my home will be next, I do not know, neither would I care so much if it were not for Daisy—poor little Daisy!— who thought she had married a rich man. The only tears I have shed over my lost fortune were for her. Oh, Daisy, Daisy!

Mary J. Holmes

CHAPTER III

EXTRACTS FROM DAISY'S JOURNAL

ELMWOOD, December 20, 18—

Daisy McDonald Thornton's journal, presented by my husband, Mr. Guy Thornton, who wishes me to write something in it every day; and when I asked him what I should write, he said: "Your thoughts, and opinions, and experiences. It will be pleasant for you some time to look back upon your early married life and see what progress you have made since then, and will help you to recall incidents you would otherwise forget. A journal fixes things in your mind, and I know you will enjoy it, especially as no one is to see it, and you can talk to it freely as to a friend."

That is what Guy said, and I wrote it right down to copy into the book as a kind of preface or introduction. I am not much pleased with having to keep a journal, and maybe I shall have Zillah keep it for me. I don't care to fix things in my mind. I don't like things fixed, anyway. I'd rather they would be round loose, as they surely would, if I had not Zillah to pick them up. She is a treasure, and it is almost worth being married to have a waiting maid—and that reminds me that I may as well begin back at the time when I was not married, and did not want to be, if only we had not been so poor, and obliged to make so many shifts to seem richer than we were.

My maiden name was Margaret McDonald, and I am seventeen next New Year's Day. My father is of Scotch descent, and a lawyer; my mother was a Barnard, from New Orleans, and has the best blood of the two. I am an only child, and very handsome—so everybody says—and I should know it if they did not say it, for can't I see myself in the glass! And still I really do not care so much for my good looks except as they serve to attain the end for which father says I was born.

Almost the first thing I can remember is of his telling me that I must marry young and marry rich, and I promised him I would, and asked if I could stay at home with mother just the same after I was married. Another thing I remember, which made a lasting impression, and that is the beating father gave me for asking before some grand people staying at our house, "Why we did not always have beefsteak and hot muffins for breakfast, instead of just baked potatoes and bread and butter."

I must learn to keep my mouth shut, father said, and not tell all I knew; and I profited by the lesson, and that is one reason, I suppose, why I so rarely say what I think, or express an opinion whether favorable or otherwise.

I do not believe I am deceitful, though all my life I have seen my parents try to seem what they are not; that is, try to seem like rich people, when sometimes father's practice brought him only a few hundreds a year, and there was mother and myself and Tom to support. Tom is my cousin—Tom McDonald—who lived with us and fell in love with me, though I never tried to make him. I liked him ever so much, though he used to tease me horribly, and put horn-bugs in my shoes, and worms on my neck, and Jack-o'-lanterns in my room, and tip me off his sled into the snow; but still I liked him, for with all his teasing he had a great, kind, unselfish heart, and I shall never forget that look on his face when I told him I could not be his wife. I did not like him as he liked me, and I did not want to be married anyway, and if I did marry it must be to some rich man. That was in Chicago, and the night before he started for South America, where he was going to make his fortune, and he wanted me to promise to wait for him, and said no one would ever love me as well as he did.

I could not promise, because, even if he had all the gold mines in Peru, I did not care to spend my days with him—to see him morning, noon, and night, and all the time. It is a good deal to ask of a woman, and I told him so, and he cried so hard—not loud, but in a pitiful kind of way, which hurt me cruelly. I hear that sobbing sometimes now in my sleep, and it's like the moan of the wind round that house on the prairie where Tom's mother died. Poor Tom! I gave him a lock of my hair and let him kiss me twice, and then he went away, and after that old Judge Burton offered himself and his million to me; but I could not endure his bald head a week, and I told him no, and when father seemed sorry and said I missed it, I told him I would not sell myself for gold alone. I'd run away first and go after Tom. Then Guy Thornton came, and—and—well, he took me by storm, and I liked him better than anyone I ever saw, and I married him. Everybody said he was rich, and father was satisfied and gave his consent, and bought be a most elaborate trousseau. I wondered then where the money came from. Now I know that Tom sent it. He has been very successful with his mine, and in a letter to father sent me a check for fifteen hundred dollars. Father would not tell me that, but mother did, and I felt worse, I think, than when I heard the sobbing. Poor Tom! I never wear one of the dresses now without thinking who paid for it and wrote, "I am working like an ox for Daisy." Poor, poor Tom!

OCTOBER 1, 18—

I rather like writing in my journal, for here I can say what I think, and I guess I shall not let Zillah make the entries. Where did I leave off? Oh, about poor Tom.

I have had a letter from him. He had just heard of my marriage, and only said: "God bless you, my darling little Daisy, and may you be very happy."

I burned the letter up and cried myself into a headache. I wish people would not love me so hard. I do not deserve it. There's Guy, my husband, more to be pitied than Tom, because, you see, he has got me; and, privately, between you and me, old journal, I am not worth the getting, and I know it perhaps better than anyone else. I like Guy and believe him to be the best man in the world, and I would rather he kissed me than Tom, but do not want anybody to kiss me; and Guy is so affectionate, and his great hands are so hot, and muss my fluted dresses so terribly.

I guess I don't like to be married anyway. If one only could have the house, and the money, and the nice things without the man! That's wicked, of course, when Guy is so kind and loves me so much. I wish he didn't, but I would not for the world let him know how I feel. I did tell him that I was not the wife he ought to have, but he would not believe me, and father was anxious, and so I married him, meaning to do the best I could. It was splendid at Saratoga, only Guy danced so ridiculously and would not let me waltz with those young men. As if I cared a straw for them or any other man besides Guy and Tom!

It is pleasant here at Elmwood, only the house is not as grand as I supposed, and there are not as many servants, and the family carriage is awful poky. Guy is to give me a pretty

Mary J. Holmes

little phaeton on my birthday.

I like Miss Frances very much, only she is such a raging housekeeper, and keeps me all the while on the alert. I don't believe in these raging housekeepers, who act as if they wanted to make the bed before you are up, and eat breakfast before it is ready. I don't like to get up in the morning anyway, and I don't like to hurry, and I am always behind, and keeping somebody waiting, and that disturbs the people here very much. Miss Frances seems really cross sometimes, and even Guy looks sober and disturbed when he has waited for me half an hour. I guess I must try and do better, for both Guy and Miss Frances are as good as they can be, but then I am not one bit like them, and have never been accustomed to anything like order and regularity. At home things came round any time, and I came with them, and that suited me better than this being married, a great deal, only now I have a kind of settled feeling, and am Mrs. Guy Thornton, and Guy is good-looking, and highly esteemed, and very learned, and I can see that the young ladies in the neighborhood envy me for being his wife. I wonder who is that Julia Hamilton Miss Frances talks about so much, and why Guy did not marry her instead of me. She, too, is very learned and gets up in the morning and flies round and reads scientific articles in the *Westminster Review*. I asked Guy once why he did not marry her instead of a little goose like me, and he said he liked the little goose the best, and then kissed me, and crumpled my white dress all up. Poor Guy! I wish I did love him as well as he does me, but it's not in me to love any man!

DECEMBER 20, 18—.

A horrible thing has happened, and I have married a poor man after all! Guy signed for somebody and had to pay, and Elmwood must be sold, and we are to move into a stuffy little house without Zillah, and with only one girl. It is too dreadful to think about, and I was sick for a week after Guy told me of it. I might as well have married Tom, only I like Guy the best. He looks so sorry and sad that I sometimes forget myself to pity him. I am going home to mother for a long, long time—all winter, maybe—and I shall enjoy it so much. Guy says I have ten thousand dollars of my own, and the interest on that will buy my dresses, I guess, and get something for Miss Frances, too. She is a noble woman, and tries to bear up so brave. She says they will keep the furniture of my blue room for me, if I want it; and I do, and I mean to have Guy send it to Indianapolis, if he will. Oh, mother, I am so glad I am coming back, and I almost wish—no, I don't, either. I like Guy, only I don't like being married!

Mary J. Holmes

CHAPTER IV

AUTHOR'S STORY

Reader, Guy Thornton was not a fool, and Daisy was not a fool, though I admit they have thus far appeared to disadvantage. Both had made a great mistake; Guy in marrying a child whose mind was unformed, and Daisy in marrying at all, when her whole nature was in revolt against matrimony. But married they are, and Guy has failed and Daisy is going home, and the New Year's morning, when she was to have received Guy's gift of the phaeton and ponies, found her at the little cottage in Indianapolis, where she at once resumed all the old indolent habits of her girlhood, and was happier than she had been since leaving home as a bride.

On the father, Mr. McDonald, the news of his son-in-law's failure fell like a thunderbolt and affected him more than it did Daisy. Shrewd, ambitious, and scheming, he had for years planned for his daughter a moneyed marriage, and now she was returned upon his hands for an indefinite time, with her naturally luxurious tastes intensified by recent indulgence, and her husband a ruined man. It was not a pleasant picture to contemplate, and Mr. McDonald's face was cloudy and thoughtful for many days until a letter from Tom turned his thoughts into a new channel and sent him with fresh avidity to certain points of law with which he had of late years been familiar. If there was one part of his profession in which he excelled more than another it was in the divorce cases which had made Indiana so notorious. Squire McDonald, as he was called, was well known to that class of people who, utterly ignoring God's command, seek to free themselves from the bonds which once were so pleasant to wear, and now, as he sat alone in his office with Tom's letter in his hand, and read how rapidly that young man was getting rich, there came into his mind a plan, the very thought of which would have made Guy Thornton shudder with horror and disgust.

Daisy had not been altogether satisfied with her brief married life, and it would be very easy to make her more dissatisfied, especially as the home to which she would return must necessarily be very different from Elmwood, Tom was destined to be a millionaire. There was no doubt of that, and once in the family he could be molded and managed as the wily McDonald had never been able to mold or manage Guy. But everything pertaining to Tom must be kept carefully out of sight, for the man knew his daughter would never lend herself to such a diabolical scheme as that which he was revolving, and which he at once put in progress, managing so adroitly that before Daisy was at all aware of what she was doing, she found herself the heroine of a divorce suit, founded really upon nothing but a general dissatisfaction with married life and a wish to be free from it. Something there was about incompatibility of temperament and uncongeniality, and all that kind of thing which wicked men and women parade before the world when weary of the tie which God has distinctly said shall not be torn asunder.

It is not our intention to follow the suit through any of its details, and we shall only say that it progressed rapidly, while poor, unsuspicious Guy was working hard to retrieve in some way his lost fortune, and to fit up a pleasant home

　　　　Mary J. Holmes

for the childish wife who was drifting away from him. He had missed her so much at first, even while he felt it a relief to have her gone just when his business matters needed all his time and thought.

It was some comfort, too, to write to her, but not much to receive her letters, for Daisy did not excel in epistolary composition, and after a few weeks her letters were short and far apart, and, as Guy thought, constrained and studied in their tone, and when, after she had been absent from him for three months or more his longing to see her was so great that he decided upon a visit of a few days to the West, and apprised her of his intention, asking if she would be glad to see him. He received in reply a telegram from Mr. McDonald telling him to defer his journey, as Daisy was visiting some friends and would be absent for an indefinite length of time. There was but one more letter from her and that was dated at Vincennes, and merely said that she was well, and Guy must not feel anxious about her or take the trouble to come to see her, as she knew how valuable his time must be and would far rather he should devote himself to his business than bother about her. The letter was signed, "Hastily, Daisy," and Guy read it over many times with a pang in his heart he could not define.

But he had no suspicion of the terrible blow in store for him, and went on planning for her comfort just the same; and when at last Elmwood was sold and he could no longer stay there, he hired a more expensive house than he could afford, because he thought Daisy would like it better, and then, with his sister Fan, set himself to the pleasant task of fitting it up for Daisy. There was a blue room with a bay window just as there had been in Elmwood, only it was not so pretentious and large. But it was very pleasant and had a door opening out upon what Guy meant should be a flower garden in the summer, and though he missed his little wife sadly and longed so much at times for a sight of her beautiful face and the sound of her sweet voice, he put all thought of himself aside and said he would not bring her back until the May flowers were in blossom and the young grass bright and green by the blue room door.

"She will have a better impression of her new home then," he said to Fan; "and I want her to be happy here and not feel the change too keenly."

Julia Hamilton chanced those days to be in town, and as she was very intimate with Miss Thornton the two were a great deal together, and it thus came about that Julia was often at the brown cottage and helped to settle the blue room for Daisy.

"If it were only you who was to occupy it," Frances said to her one morning when they had been reading together for an hour or more in the room they both thought so pleasant. "I like Daisy, but somehow she seems so far from me. Why, there's not a sentiment in common between us."

Then, as if sorry for having said so much, she spoke of Daisy's marvelous beauty and winning ways, and hoped Julia would know and love her ere long, and possibly do her good.

It so happened that Guy was sometimes present at these readings, enjoying them so much that there insensibly crept into his heart a wish that Daisy was more like the Boston girl whom he had mentally termed strong-minded.

"And in time, perhaps, she may be," he thought. "I mean to have Julia here a great deal next summer, and with two such women for companions as Julia and Fan, Daisy cannot help but improve."

And so at last, when the house was settled and the early spring flowers were in bloom, Guy started westward for his wife. He had not seen her now for months, and it was more than two weeks since he had heard from her, and his heart beat high with joyful anticipation as he thought just how she would look when she came to him, shyly and coyly, as she always did, with that droop in her eyelids and that pink flush in her cheeks. He would chide her a little at first, he said, for having been so poor a correspondent, especially of late, and after that he would love her so much, and shield her so tenderly from every want or care, that she should never feel the difference in his fortune.

Poor Guy—he little dreamed what was in store for him just inside the door where he stood ringing one morning early in May, and which, when at last it was opened, shut in a very different man from the one who went through it three hours later, benumbed and half-crazed with bewilderment and surprise.

CHAPTER V

THE DIVORCE

He had expected to meet Daisy in the hall, but she was nowhere in sight, and she who appeared in response to the card he sent up seemed confused and unnatural to such a degree that Guy asked in some alarm if anything had happened, and where Daisy was.

Nothing had happened—that is—well, nothing was the matter with Daisy, Mrs. McDonald said, only she was nervous and not feeling quite well that morning, and thought she had better not come down. They had not expected him so soon, she continued, and she regretted exceedingly that her husband was not there, but she had sent for him, and hoped he would come immediately. Had Mr. Thornton been to breakfast?

Yes, he had, and he did not understand at all what she meant; if Daisy could not come to him he must go to her, he said, and he started for the door, when Mrs. McDonald sprang forward, and, laying her hand on his arm, held him back, saying:

"Wait, Mr. Thornton; wait till husband comes—to tell you—"

Mary J. Holmes

"Tell me what?" Guy demanded of her, feeling sure now that something had befallen Daisy.

"Tell you—that—that—Daisy is—that he has—that—oh, believe me, it was not my wish, and I don't know now why it was done," Mrs. McDonald said, still trying to detain Guy and keep him in the room.

But her efforts were vain, for, shaking off her grasp, Guy opened the hall door, and with a cry of joy caught Daisy herself in his arms.

In a state of fearful excitement and very curious to know what was passing between her mother and Guy, she had stolen downstairs to listen, and had reached the door just as Guy opened it so suddenly.

"Daisy, darling, I feared you were sick," he cried, nearly smothering her with his caresses.

But Daisy writhed herself away from him, and, putting up her hands to keep him off, cried out:

"Oh, Guy, Guy, you can't—you mustn't. You must never kiss me again or love me any more, because I am—I am not—oh, Guy, I wish you had never seen me; I am so sorry, too. I did like you. I—I—Guy—Guy—I ain't your wife any more! Father has got a divorce!"

She whispered the last words, and then, affrighted at the expression of Guy's face, fled half-way up the stairs, where she stood looking down upon him, while, with a face as white as ashes, he, too, stood gazing at her and trying to frame the words which should ask her what she meant. He did not believe her literally; the idea was too preposterous, but he felt that something horrible had come between him and Daisy—that in some way she was as much lost to him as if he had found her coffined for the grave, and the suddenness of the blow took from him for a moment his powers of speech, and he still stood looking at her when the street door opened and a new actor appeared upon the scene in the person of Mr. McDonald, who had hastened home in obedience to the message from his wife.

It was a principle of Mr. McDonald never to lose his presence of mind or his temper, or the smooth, low tone of voice he had cultivated years ago and practiced since with so good effect. And now, though he understood the state of matters at once and knew that Guy had heard the worst, he did not seem ruffled in the slightest degree, and his voice was just as kind and sweet as ever as he bade Guy good-morning and advanced to shake his hand. But Guy would not take it. He had always disliked and distrusted Mr. McDonald, and he felt intuitively that whatever harm had befallen him had come through the oily-tongued, insinuating man who stood smilingly before him. With a gesture of disgust he turned away from the offered hand, and in a voice husky with suppressed excitement, asked:

"What does all this mean, that when, after a separation of months, I come for my wife I am told that she is not my wife—that there has been a—a divorce?"

Guy had brought himself to name the horrid thing, and the very sound of the word served to make it more real and clear to his mind, and there were great drops of sweat upon his forehead and about his mouth as he asked what it meant.

"Oh, Guy, don't feel so badly. Tell him, father, I did not do it," Daisy cried, as she stood leaning over the stair-rail and looking down at the wretched man.

Mary J. Holmes

"Daisy, go to your room. You should not have seen him at all," Mr. McDonald said, with more sternness of manner than was usual for him.

Then, turning to Guy, he continued:

"Come in here, Mr. Thornton, where we can be alone while I explain to you what seems so mysterious now."

They went together into the little parlor, and for half an hour or more the sound of their voices was distinctly heard as Mr. McDonald tried to explain what there really was no explanation or excuse for. Daisy was not contented at Elmwood, and though she complained of nothing, she was not happy as a married woman, and was glad to be free again. That was all, and Guy understood at last that Daisy was his no longer; that the law which was a disgrace to the State in which it existed had divorced him from his wife without his knowledge or consent, and for no other reason than incompatibility of temperament, and a desire on Daisy's part to be free from the marriage tie. Not a word had been said of Guy's altered fortunes, but he felt that his comparative poverty was really the cause of this great wrong, and for a few moments resentment and indignation prevailed over every other feeling; then, when he remembered the little blue-eyed, innocent-faced girl whom he had loved so much and thought so good and true, he laid his head upon the sofa arm and groaned bitterly, while the man who had ruined him sat coolly by, citing to him many similar cases where divorces had been procured without the knowledge of the absent party. It was a common—a very common thing, he said, and reflected no disgrace upon either party where there was no criminal charge. Daisy was too young and childish anyway, and ought not to have been married for several years, and it was really quite as much a favor to Guy as a wrong. He was free again—free to marry if he liked—he had taken care to see to that, so—

"Stop!" Guy almost thundered out. "There is a point beyond which you shall not go. Be satisfied with taking Daisy from me, and do not insult me with talk of a second marriage. Had I found Daisy dead it would have hurt me less than this fearful wrong you have done. I say you, for I charge it all to you. Daisy could have had no part in it, and I ask to see her and hear from her own lips that she accepts the position in which you and your diabolical laws have placed her before I am willing to give her up. Call her, will you?"

"No, Mr. Thornton," Mr. McDonald replied. "To see Daisy would be useless and only excite you more than you are excited now. You cannot see her."

"Yes, he will, father. If Guy wants to see me, he shall."

It was Daisy herself who spoke, and who a second time had been acting the part of listener. Going up to Guy, she knelt down beside him, and, laying her arms across his lap, said to him:

"What is it, Guy? what is it you wish to say to me?"

The sight of her before him in all her girlish beauty, with that soft, sweet expression on the face raised so timidly to his, unmanned Guy entirely, and, clasping her in his arms, he wept passionately for a moment, while he tried to say:

"Oh, Daisy, my darling, tell me it is a horrid dream; tell me you are still my wife, and go with me to the home I have tried to make so pleasant for your sake. It is not like Elmwood, but I will some time have one handsomer even than that, and I'll work so hard for you! Oh, Daisy, tell me you are sorry for the part you had in this fearful business, if, indeed, you had a part, and I'll take you back so gladly! Will you, Daisy? will you be my wife once more? I shall never ask you again. This is your last chance with me. Reflect before you throw it away."

Guy's mood was changing a little, because of something he saw in Daisy's face—a drawing back from him when he spoke of marriage.

"Daisy must not go back with you; I shall not suffer that," Mr. McDonald said, while Daisy, still keeping her arms around Guy's neck, where she had put them when he drew her to him, replied:

"Oh, Guy! I can't go with you now; but I shall like you always, and I'm so sorry for you. I never wanted to be married; but if I must, I'd better have married Tom, or that old Chicago man; they would not feel so bad, and I'd rather hurt them than you."

The utter childishness of the remark roused Guy, and with a gesture of impatience, he put Daisy from him, and, rising to his feet, said angrily:

"This, then is your decision, and I accept it; but, Daisy, if you have in you a spark of true womanhood you will some time be sorry for this day's work; while you!" and he turned fiercely upon Mr. McDonald—"words cannot express the contempt I feel for you; and know, too, that I understand you fully, and am certain that were I the rich man I was when you gave your daughter to me, you would not have taken her away. But I will waste no more words upon you. You are a villain! and Daisy is—" His white lips quivered a little as he hesitated a moment, and then added: "Daisy was my wife."

Then, without another word, he left the house, nor saw the white, frightened face which looked after him so wistfully until a turn in the street hid him from view.

CHAPTER VI

EXTRACTS FROM DIARIES

Extract 1st—Mr. McDonald's.

MAY—

Well, that matter is over, and I can't say I am sorry, for the expression in that Thornton's eye I do not care to meet a second time. There was mischief in it, and it made one think of six-shooters and cold lead. I never quite indorsed the man—first, because he was not as rich as I would like Daisy's husband to be, and, second, because even if he had been a millionaire it would have done me no good. That he did not marry Daisy's family, he made me fully understand, and for any good his money did me, I was as poor after the marriage as before. Then he must needs lose all he had in that foolish way, and when I found that Daisy was not exceedingly in love with married life, it was natural that, as her father, I should take advantage of the laws of the State in which I live, especially as Tom is growing rich so fast. On the whole, I have done a good thing. Daisy is free, with ten thousand dollars that Thornton settled on her, for, of course, I shall prevent her giving that back, as she is determined to do, saying it is not hers, and she will not keep it. It is hers, and she shall keep it, and Tom will be a millionaire if that gold mine proves as great a success as it seems now to be, and I can manage Tom, and, as I said before, I've done a nice thing after all.

Extract 2nd—Miss Thornton's.

JUNE 30, 18—

To-day, for the first time, we have hopes that my brother will live; but, oh! how near he has been to the gates of death since that night when he came back to us from the West, with a fearful look on his face and a cruel stab in his heart. I say us, for Julia Hamilton has been with me all through the dreadful days and nights when I watched to see Guy's life go out and know I was left alone. She was with me when I was getting ready for Daisy and waiting for Guy to bring her home—not to Elmwood—that dear old place is sold and strangers walk the rooms I love so well—but here to the brown cottage on the hill, which, if I had never had Elmwood, would seem so pleasant to me.

And it is pleasant here, especially in Daisy's room, which we shall never use, for the door is shut and bolted, and it seems each time I pass it as if a dead body were inside. Had Guy died I would have laid him there and sent for that false creature to come and see her work. I promised her so much, but not from any love, for my heart was full of bitterness that night when I turned her from the door out into the rain. I shall never tell Guy that—never, lest he should soften toward her, and I would not have her here again for all the world contains. And yet I did like her, and was looking forward to her return with a good deal of pleasure. Julia had spoken many a kind word for her, had pleaded her extreme youth as an excuse for her faults, and had led me to hope for better things when time had matured her somewhat and she had become accustomed to our new mode of life.

And so I hoped and waited for her and Guy, and wondered I did not hear from him, and felt so glad and happy when I received the telegram, "Shall be home to-night." It was a bright day in May, but the evening set in cool, with a feeling of rain in the air, and I had a fire kindled in the parlor and in Daisy's room, for I remembered how she used to crouch on the rug before the grate and watch the blaze floating up the chimney with all the eagerness of a child. Then, although it hurt me sorely, I went to Simpson, who bought our carriage, and asked that it might be sent to the station so that Daisy should not feel the difference at once. And Jerry, our old coachman, went with it and waited there just as Julia and I waited at home, for Julia had promised to stay a few weeks and see what Daisy was like.

The train was late that night, an hour behind time, and the spring rain was falling outside and the gas was lighted within when I heard the sound of wheels stopping at the door and went to meet my brother. But only my brother. There was no Daisy with him. He came in alone, with such an awful look on his white face as made me cry out with alarm.

"What it is, Guy, and where is Daisy?" I asked, as he staggered against the banister, where he leaned heavily.

He did not answer my question, but said, "Take me to my room," in a voice I would never have known for Guy's. I took him to his room, made him lie down, and brought him a glass of wine, and then, when he was strong enough to tell it, listened to the shameful story, and felt that henceforth and forever I must and would hate the woman who had wounded my Guy so cruelly.

And still there is some good in her—some sense of right and wrong, as was shown by a strange thing which happened when Guy was at the worst of the terrible fever which followed his coming home. I watched him day and night, I would not even let Julia Hamilton share my vigils, and one night when I was worn out with fatigue and anxiety I fell asleep upon the lounge, where I threw myself for a moment. How long I slept I never knew, but it must have been an hour or more, for the last thing I remember was hearing the whistle of the Western train and the sighing of the wind, which sounded like rain, and when I awoke the rain was falling heavily and the clock was striking twelve, which was an hour after the train was due. It was very quiet in the room, and darker than usual, for someone had shaded the lamp from my eyes as well as Guy's so that at first I did not see distinctly, but I had an impression that there was a figure sitting by Guy near the bed. Julia, most likely, I thought, and I called her by name, feeling my blood curdle in my veins and my heart stand still with something like fear when a voice I knew so well and never expected to hear again, answered softly:

"It is not Julia. It's me!"

There was no faltering in her voice, no sound of apology. She spoke like one who had a right there, and this it was which angered me and made me lose my self-command. Starting to my feet, I confronted her where she sat in my chair, by Guy's bedside, with those queer blue eyes of hers fixed so questioningly upon me as if she wondered at my impertinence.

"Miss McDonald," I said, laying great stress on the name, "why are you here, and how did you dare come?"

"I was almost afraid, it was so dark when I left the train, and it kept thundering so," she replied, mistaking my meaning altogether, "but there was no conveyance at the station, and so I came on alone. I never knew Guy was sick. Is he very bad?"

Her perfect composure and utter ignoring of the past provoked me beyond endurance, and without stopping to think what I was doing, I seized her arm, and drawing her into an adjoining room, said, in a suppressed whisper of rage:

"Very bad—I should think so. We have feared and still fear he will die, and it's all your work, the result of your wickedness, and yet you presume to come here into his very room—you who are no wife of his, and no woman, either, to do what you have done."

What more I said I do not remember. I only know Daisy put her hands to her head in a scared, helpless way, and said:

"I do not quite understand it all, or what you wish me to do."

"Do?" I replied. "I want you to leave this house to-night— now, before Guy can possibly be harmed by your presence. Go back to the depot and take the next train home. It is due in an hour. You have time to reach it."

"But it's so dark, and it rains and thunders so," she said, with a shudder, as a heavy peal shook the house and the rain beat against the windows.

I think I must have been crazy with mad excitement, and her answer made me worse.

"You were not afraid to come here," I said. "You can go from here as well. Thunder will not hurt such as you."

Even then she did not move, but crouched in a corner of the room farthest from me, reminding me of my kitten when I try to drive it from a place where it has been permitted to play. As that will not understand my scats and gestures, so she did not seem to comprehend my meaning. But I made her at last, and with a very white face and a strange look in her great, staring blue eyes, she said:

"Fanny" (she always called me Miss Frances before), "Fanny, do you really mean me to go back in the dark and the rain and the thunder? Then I will, but I must tell you first what I came for, and you will tell Guy. He gave me ten thousand dollars when we first were married; settled it on me, they called it, and father was one of the trustees and kept the paper for me till I was of age. So much I understand, but not why I can't give it back to Guy, for father says I can't. I never dreamed it was mine after the—the—the divorce."

She spoke the word softly and hesitatingly, while a faint flush showed on her otherwise white face.

"If I am not Guy's wife, as they say, then I have no right to his money, and I told father so, and said I'd give it back, and he said I couldn't, and I said I could and would, and I wrote to Guy about it, told him I was not so mean, and father kept the letter, and I did not know what I should do next till I was invited to visit Aunt Merriman in Detroit. Then I took the paper—the settlement, you know, from the box where father kept it and put it in my pocket; here it is—see," and she drew out a document and held it toward me while she continued: "I started for Detroit under the care of a friend who stopped a few miles the other side, so you see I was free to come here if I liked, and I did so, for I wanted to see Guy and give him the paper, and tell him I'd never take a cent of his money. I am sorry he is sick. I did not think he'd care so much, and I don't know what to do with the paper unless I tear it up. I believe I'd better; then, surely, it will be out of the way."

　　　　Mary J. Holmes

And before I could speak or think she tore the document in two, and then across again, and scattered the four pieces on the floor.

"Tell Guy, please," she continued, "what I have done, and that I never meant to take it, after—after—that—you know —and that I did not care for money only as father taught me I must have it, and that I am sorry he ever saw me, and I never really wanted to be married and can't be his wife again till I do."

She spoke as if Guy would take her back of course if she only signified her wish to come, and this kept me angry, though I was beginning to soften a little with this unexpected phase of her character, and I might have suffered her to stay till morning if she had signified a wish to do so, but she did not.

"I suppose I must go now if I would catch the train," she said, moving toward the door. "Good-by, Fanny. I am sorry I ever troubled you."

She held her little white, ungloved hand toward me, and then I came to myself, and, hearing the wind and rain, and remembering the lonely road to the station, I said to her:

"Stay, Daisy, I cannot let you go alone. Miss Hamilton will watch with Guy while I go with you."

"And who will go with you? It will be just as dark and rainy then," she said; but she made no objection to my plan, and in less than five minutes Julia, who always slept in her dressing-gown so as to be ready for any emergency, was sitting by Guy, and I was out in the dark night with Daisy and our watchdog Leo, who, at sight of his old playmate, had leaped upon her and nearly knocked her down in his joy.

"Leo is glad to see me," Daisy said, patting the dumb creature's head, and in her voice there was a rebuking tone, which I resented silently.

I was not glad to see her, and I could not act a part, but I wrapped my waterproof around her and adjusted the hood over her flowing hair, and thought how beautiful she was, even in that disfiguring garb, and then we went on our way, the young creature clinging close to me as peal after peal of thunder rolled over our heads, and gleams of lightning lit up the inky sky. She did not speak to me, nor I to her, till the red light on the track was in sight, and we knew the train was coming. Then she asked timidly. "Do you think Guy will die?"

"Heaven only knows," I said, checking a strong impulse to add: "If he does, you will have the satisfaction of knowing that you killed him."

I was glad now that I did not say it. And I was glad then, when Daisy, alarmed perhaps by something in the tone of my voice, repeated her question:

"But do you think he will die? If I thought he would I should wish to die, too. I like him, Miss Frances, better than anyone I ever saw; like him now as well as I ever did, but I do not want to be his wife, nor anybody's wife, and that is just the truth. I am sorry he ever saw me and loved me so well. Tell him that, Fanny."

It was Fanny again and she grasped my hand nervously, for the train was upon us.

"Promise me solemnly that if you think he is surely going to die you will let me know in time to see him once more. Promise—quick—and kiss me as a pledge."

Mary J. Holmes

The train had stopped. There was not a moment to lose, and I promised, and kissed the red lips in the darkness, and felt a remorseful pang when I saw the little figure go alone into the car which bore her swiftly away, while I turned my steps homeward with only Leo for my companion.

I had to tell Julia about it, and I gathered up the four scraps of paper from the floor where Daisy had thrown them, and, joining them together, saw they really were the marriage settlement, and kept them for Guy, should he ever be able to hear about it and know what it meant. There was a telegram for me the next evening, dated at Detroit, and bearing simply the words, "Arrived safely," and that was all I heard of Daisy. No one in town knew of her having been here but Julia and myself, and it was better that they should not, for Guy's life hung on a thread, and for many days and nights I trembled lest that promise, sealed by a kiss, would have to be redeemed.

That was three weeks ago, and Guy is better now and knows us all, and to-day, for the first time, I have a strong hope that I am not to be left alone, and I thank Heaven for that hope, and feel as if I were at peace with all the world, even with Daisy herself, from whom I have heard nothing since that brief telegram.

AUGUST 1,—

The shadow of death has passed from our house, and I may almost say the shadow of sickness, too, for though Guy is still weak as a child and thin as a ghost, he is decidedly on the gain, and to-day I drove him out for the third time, and felt from something he said that he was beginning to feel some interest in the life so kindly given back to him. Still he will never be just the same. The blow stunned him too completely for him to recover quite his old hopeful, happy manner, and there is a look of age in his face which pains me to see. He knows Daisy has been here, and why. I had to tell him all about it, and sooner, too, than I meant. Almost his first coherent question to me after his reason came back was:

"Where is Daisy? I am sure I heard her voice. It could not have been a dream. Is she here, or has she been here? Tell me the truth, Fanny."

So I told him, though I did not mean to, and showed him the bits of paper, and held his head on my bosom while he cried like a little child. How he loves her yet, and how glad he was to know that she was not as mercenary as it would at first seem. Not that her tearing up that paper will make any difference about the money. She cannot give it to him, he says, until she is of age, neither does he wish it at all, and he would not take it from her; but he is glad to see her disposition in the matter; glad to have me think better of her than I did, and I am certain that he is half expecting to hear from her every day and is disappointed that he does not. He did not reproach me when I told him about turning her out in the rain; he only said:

"Poor Daisy, did she get very wet? She is so delicate, you know. I hope it did not make her sick."

Oh, the love a man will feel for a woman, let her be ever so unworthy. I cannot comprehend it. And why should I—an old maid like me, who never loved anyone but Guy?

AUGUST 30,—

In a roundabout way we have heard that Mr. McDonald is going away with his wife and daughter. When the facts of the divorce were known they brought him into such disgrace with the citizens of Indianapolis that he thought it best to leave for a time till the storm blows over, and so they will go to South America, where there is a cousin Tom, who is growing rich very fast. I cannot help certain thoughts coming into my mind any more than I can help being glad that Daisy is going out of the country. Guy never mentions her now, and is getting to look and act quite like himself. If only he could forget her we might be very happy again, as Heaven grant we may.

CHAPTER VII

FIVE YEARS LATER

"Married, this morning, at St. Paul's Church, by the Rev. Dr.—, assisted by the rector, Guy Thornton, Esq., of Cuylerville, to Miss Julia Hamilton, of this city."

Such was the notice which appeared in a daily Boston paper one lovely morning in September five years after the last entry in Miss Thornton's journal. Guy had reached the point at last when he could put Daisy from his heart and take another in her place. He had never seen her or heard directly from her since the night she brought him the marriage settlement and tore it in pieces, thinking thus to give it to him beyond a doubt. That this did not change the matter one whit he knew just as he knew she could not give him the ten thousand dollars settled upon her until she was of age. She was of age now, and had been for a year or more, and, to say the truth, he had expected to hear from her when she was twenty-one. To himself he had reasoned in this wise: Her father told her that the tearing up that paper made no difference, that she was powerless of herself to act until she was of age, so she will wait quietly till then before making another effort. And in his heart Guy thought how he would not take a penny from her, but would insist upon her keeping it. Still he should respect her all the more for her sense of

Mary J. Holmes

justice and generosity, he thought, and when her twenty-first birthday came and passed, and week after week went by, and brought no sign from Daisy, there was a pang in his heart and a look of disappointment on his face which did not pass away until October hung her gorgeous colors upon the hills of Cuylerville, and Julia Hamilton came to the Brown Cottage to spend a few weeks with his sister.

From an independent, self-reliant, energetic girl of twenty-two Julia had ripened into a noble and dignified woman of twenty-seven, with a quiet repose of manner which seemed to rest and quiet one, and which told insensibly on Guy, until at last he found himself dreading to have her go and wishing to keep her with him always. The visit was lengthened into a month; and when in November he went with her to Boston he had asked her to take Daisy's place, and she had said she would. Very freely they had talked of the little golden-haired girl, and Julia told him what she had heard of her through a mutual acquaintance who had been on the same vessel with the McDonalds when they returned from South America. Cousin Tom was with them, a rich man then and a richer now, for his gold mine and his railroad had made him almost a millionaire, and it was currently reported and believed that Mr. McDonald designed him for his daughter. They were abroad now, the McDonalds and Tom, who bore the expenses of the party. Daisy, it was said, was even more beautiful than in her early girlhood, and to her loveliness were added cultivation and refinement of manner. She had had the best of teachers while in South America, and was now continuing her studies abroad with a view to further improvement. All this Julia Hamilton told Guy, and then bade him think again ere deciding to join her life with his.

And Guy did think again, and his thoughts went across the sea after the beautiful Daisy, and he tried to picture to himself what she must be, now that education and culture had set their seal upon her. But always in the picture there was a dark background, where cousin Tom stood sentinel with his bags of gold, and so, with a half-unconscious sigh for what "might have been," Guy dug still deeper the grave where years before he had buried his love for Daisy, and to make the burial sure this time, so that there should be no future resurrection, he put over the grave a head-stone on which were written a new hope and a new love, both of which centered in Julia Hamilton. And so they were engaged, and after that there was no wavering on his part— no looking back to a past which seemed like a happy dream from which there had been a horrible awaking.

He loved Julia at first quietly and sensibly, and loved her more and more as the winter and spring went by and brought the day when he stood again at the altar and for the second time took upon him the marriage vow. It was a very quiet wedding, with only a few friends present, and Miss Frances was the bridesmaid, in a gown of silver gray; but Julia's face was bright with the certainty of a happiness long desired; and if in Guy's heart there lingered the odor of other bridal flowers, withered now and dead, and the memory of other marriage bells than those which sent their music on the air that summer morning, and if a pair of sunny blue eyes looked into his instead of Julia's darker ones, he made no sign, and his face wore an expression of perfect content as he took his second bride for better or worse, just as he once had taken little Daisy. In her case it had proved all for the worse, but now there was a suitableness in the union which boded future happiness, and many a hearty wish for good was sent after the newly married pair, whose destination was New York.

It was nearly dark when they reached the hotel and quite dark before dinner was over. Then Julia suddenly remembered that an old friend of hers was boarding in the house, and suggested going to her room.

"I'd send my card," she said blushingly, "only she would not know me by the new name, so if you do not mind my leaving you a moment I'll go and find her myself."

Guy did not mind, and Julia went out and left him alone. Scarcely was she gone when he called to mind a letter which had been forwarded to him from Cuylerville, and which he had found awaiting him on his return from the church. Not thinking it of much consequence he had thrust it in his pocket and in the excitement forgotten it till now. He had dressed for dinner and worn his wedding coat, and he took the letter out and looked at it a moment, and wondered whom it was from, as people ofttimes do wait and wonder, when breaking the seal would settle the wonder so soon. It was postmarked in New York, and felt heavy in his hand, and he opened it at last and found that the outer envelope inclosed another one on which his name and address were written in a handwriting once so familiar to him, and the sight of which made him start and breathe heavily for a moment as if the air had suddenly grown thick and burdensome.

Daisy's handwriting! which he had never thought to see again; for after his engagement with Julia he had burned every vestige of a correspondence it was sorrow now to remember. One by one, and with a steady hand, he had dropped Daisy's letters into the fire and watched them turning into ashes, and thought how like his love for her they were when nothing remained of them but the thin gray tissue his breath could blow away. The four scraps of the marriage settlement which Daisy had brought him on that night of storm he kept, because they seemed to embody something good and noble in the girl; but the letters she had written him were gone past recall, and he had thought himself cut loose from her forever—when, lo! there had come to him an awakening to the bitterness of the past in a letter from the once-loved wife, whose delicate handwriting made him grow faint and sick for a moment as he held the letter in his hand and read thereon:

"GUY THORNTON, ESQ.,
Brown Cottage,
Cuylerville, Mass.
Politeness of Mr. Wilkes."

Why had she written, and what had she to say to him, he wondered, and for a moment he felt tempted to tear the letter up and never know what it contained.

Better, perhaps, had he done so—better for him, and better for the fond new wife whose happiness was so perfect, and whose trust in his love so strong.

But he did not tear it up. He opened it and read—another chapter will tell us what he read.

CHAPTER VIII

DAISY'S LETTER

It was dated at Rouen, France, and it ran as follows:

"MAY 15, 18—

"DEAR, DEAR GUY:—I am all alone here in Rouen; not a person near me who speaks English or knows a thing of Daisy Thornton as she was, or as she is now, for I am Daisy Thornton here. I have taken the old name again, and am an English governess in a wealthy French family; and this is how it came about: I have left Berlin and the party there and am earning my own living for three reasons, two of which concern cousin Tom and one of which has to do with you and that miserable settlement which has troubled me so much. I thought when I brought it back and tore it up that was the last of it, and did not know that by no act of mine could I give it to you until I was of age. Father missed it, of course, and I told him just the truth, and that I could never touch a penny of your money and I not your wife. He did not say a word, and I supposed it was all right, and never dreamed that I was actually clothed and fed on the interest of that ten thousand dollars. Father would not tell me and you did not write. Why didn't you, Guy? I expected a letter so long, and went to the office so many times and cried a little to myself, and said Guy has forgotten me.

"Then we went to South Africa—father, mother, and I—went to live with Tom. He wanted me before you did, you know, but I could not marry Tom. He is very rich now, and we lived with him; and then we all came to Europe and have traveled everywhere, and I have had teachers in everything, and people say I am a fine scholar and praise me much; and, Guy, I have tried to improve just to please you; believe me, Guy, just to please you. Tom was as a brother—a dear, good big bear of a brother whom I loved as such, but nothing more. Even were you dead, I could not marry Tom after knowing you; and I told him so when in Berlin he asked me for the sixth time to be his wife. I had to tell him something hard to make him understand, and when I saw how what I said hurt him cruelly and made him cry—because he was such a great, big, awkward, dear old fellow, I put my arms around his neck and cried with him, and tried to explain, and that made him ten times worse. Oh, if folks only would not love me so it would save me so much sorrow.

"You see, I tell you this because I want you to know exactly what I have been doing these five years, and that I have never thought of marrying Tom or anybody. I did not think I could. I felt that if I belonged to anybody it was you, and I cannot have Tom; and father was very angry and taunted me with living on Tom's money, which I did not know before, and he accidentally let out about the marriage settlement, and that hurt me worse than the other.

"Oh, Guy, how can I give it up? Surely there must be a way, now I am of age. I was so humiliated about it, and after all that passed between father and Tom and me I could not stay in Berlin and never be sure whose money was paying for my bread, and when I heard that Madame Lafarcade, a French lady, who had spent the winter in Berlin, was wanting an

English governess for her children, I went to her, and, as the result, am here at this beautiful country-seat, just out of the city, earning my own living and feeling so proud to do it; only, Guy, there is an ache in my heart, a heavy, throbbing pain which will not leave me day or night, and this is how it came there.

"Mother wrote that you were about to marry Miss Hamilton. Letters from home brought her the news, which she thinks is true. Oh, Guy, it is not, it cannot be true! You must not go quite away from me now just as I am coming back to you. For, Guy, I am—or rather, I have come, and a great love, such as I never felt before, fills me full almost to bursting. I always liked you, Guy; but when we were married I did not know what it was to love—to feel my pulses quicken as they do just now at thought of you. If I had, how happy I could have made you, but I was a silly little girl, and married life was distasteful to me, and I was willing to be free, though always, way down in my heart, was something which protested against it, and if you knew just how I was influenced and led on insensibly to assent, you would not blame me so much. The word divorce had an ugly sound to me, and I did not like it, and I have always felt as if bound to you just the same. It would not be right for me to marry Tom, even if I wanted to, which I do not. I am yours, Guy— only yours, and all these years I have studied and improved for your sake, without any fixed idea, perhaps, as to what I expected or hoped. But when Tom spoke the last time it came to me suddenly what I was keeping myself for, and, just as a great body of water, when freed from its prison walls, rolls rapidly down a green meadow, so did a mighty love for you take possession of me and permeate my whole being until every nerve quivered for joy, and when Tom was gone I went away alone and cried more for my new happiness, I am afraid, than for him, poor fellow. And yet I pitied him, too; as I could not stay in Berlin after that I came away to earn money enough to take me back to you. For I am coming, or I was before I heard that dreadful news which I cannot believe.

"Is it true, Guy? Write and tell me it is not, and that you love me still and want me back, or, if it in part is true, and you are engaged to Julia, show her this letter and ask her to give you up, even if it is the very day before the wedding—for you are mine, and, sometimes, when the children are troublesome, and I am so tired and sorry and homesick, I have such a longing for a sight of your dear face, and think if I could only lay my aching head in your lap once more I should never know pain or weariness again.

"Try me, Guy. I will be so good and loving and make you so happy—and your sister, too—I was a bother to her once. I'll be a comfort now. Tell her so, please; tell her to bid me come. Say the word yourself, and, almost before you know it, I'll be there.

"Truly, lovingly, waitingly, your wife, DAISY.

"P.S.—To make sure of this letter's safety I shall send it to New York by a friend, who will mail it to you.

"Again, lovingly. DAISY THORNTON."

This was Daisy's letter which Guy read with such a pang in his heart as he had never known before, even when he was smarting the worst from wounded love and disappointed hopes. Then he had said to himself, "I can never suffer again as I am suffering now," and now, alas, he felt how little he knew of that pain which rends the heart and takes the breath away.

"God help her!" he moaned, his first thought, his first prayer, for Daisy, the girl who called herself his wife, when just across the hall, only a few rods away, was the bride of a few hours—another woman who bore his name and called him her husband.

With a face as pale as ashes and hands which shook like palsied hands, he read again that pathetic cry from her whom he now felt he had never ceased to love; aye, whom he loved still, and whom, if he could, he would have taken to his arms so gladly and loved and cherished as the priceless thing he had once thought her to be. The first moments of agony which followed the reading of the letter were Daisy's wholly, and in bitterness of soul the man she had cast off and thought to take again cried out, as he stretched his arms toward an invisible form: "Too late, darling—too late. But had it come two months, one month, or even one week ago, I would—would—have gone to you over land and sea, but now—another is in your place, another is my wife; Julia—poor, innocent Julia. God help me to keep my vow; God help me in my need!"

He was praying now; Julia was the burden of his prayer. And as he prayed there came into his heart an unutterable tenderness and pity for her. He had thought he loved her an hour ago! he believed he loved her now, or, if he did not, he would be to her the kindest, most thoughtful of husbands, and never let her know, by word or sign, of the terrible pain he should always carry in his heart. "Darling Daisy; poor Julia!" was what to himself he designated the two women who were both so much to him. To the first his love, to the other his tender care, for she was worthy of it. She was noble, and good, and womanly; he said it many times, and tried to stop the rapid heart throbs and quiet himself down to meet her when she should come to him with her frank, open face and smile, in which there was no shadow of guile. She was coming now; he heard her voice in the hall speaking to her friend, and, thrusting the fatal letter in his pocket, he rose to his feet, and steadying himself upon the table stood waiting for her, as, flushed and eager, she came in.

"Guy—Guy—what is it? Are you sick?" she asked, alarmed at the pallor on his face and the strange expression of his eyes.

He was glad she had thus construed his agitation, and he answered that he was faint and a little sick.

"It came on suddenly, while I was sitting here. It will pass off as suddenly," he said, trying to smile, and holding out his hand, which she took at once in hers.

"Is it your heart, Guy? Do you think it is your heart?" she continued, as she rubbed and caressed his cold, clammy hand.

A shadow of pain or remorse flitted across Guy's face as he replied:

"I think it is my heart, but I assure you there is no danger—the worst is over. I am a great deal better."

And he was better with that fair girl beside him, her face glowing with excitement and her soft hands pressing his. Perfectly healthy herself, she must have imparted some life and vigor to him, for he felt his pulse grow steadier beneath her touch, and the blood flow more easily through his veins.

If only he could forget that crumpled letter which lay in his vest pocket and seemed to burn into his flesh; forget that and the young girl across the sea, watching for an answer and the one word "Come!" he might be happy yet, for Julia was one whom any man could love and be proud to call his wife. And

Mary J. Holmes

Guy said to himself that he did love her, though not as he once loved Daisy, or as he could love her again were he free to do so, and because of that full love withheld he made a mental vow that his whole life should be given to her happiness, so that she might never know any care or sorrow from which he could shield her.

"And Daisy?" something whispered in his ear.

"I must and will forget her," he sternly answered, and the arm he had thrown around Julia, who was sitting with him upon the sofa, tightened its grasp until she winced and moved a little from him.

He was very talkative that evening, and asked his wife many questions about her friends and the shopping she wished to do, and the places they were to visit; and Julia, who had hitherto regarded him as a great, silent man, given to few words, wondered at the change, and watched the bright red spots on his cheeks, and thought how she would manage to have medical advice for that dreadful heart disease which had come like a nightmare to haunt her bridal days.

Next morning there came a Boston paper containing a notice of the marriage, and this Guy sent to Daisy, with only the faint tracing of a pencil to indicate the paragraph. "Better so than to write," he thought; though he longed to add the words, "Forgive me, Daisy; your letter came too late."

And so the paper was sent, and after a week or two Guy went back to his home in Cuylerville, and the blue rooms which Julia had fitted up for Daisy five years before became her own by right. And Fanny Thornton welcomed her warmly to the house, and by many little acts of thoughtfulness showed how glad she was to have her there. And Julia was very happy save when she remembered the heart disease, which she was sure Guy had, and for which he would not seek advice. "There was nothing the matter with his heart unless it were too full of love," he told her laughingly, and wondered to himself if in saying this to her he was guilty of a lie, inasmuch as his words misled her so completely.

After a time, however, there came a change, and thoughts of Daisy ceased to disturb him as they once had done. No one ever mentioned her to him, and since the receipt of her letter he had heard no tidings of her until six months after his marriage, when there came to him the ten thousand dollars, with all the interest which had accrued since the settlement first was made. There was no word from Daisy herself, but a letter from a lawyer in Berlin, who said all there was to say with regard to the business, but did not tell where Miss McDonald, as he called her, was.

Then Guy wrote to Daisy a letter of thanks, to which there came no reply, and as time went on the old wound began to heal, the grave to close again; and when, at last, one year after his marriage, they brought him a beautiful little baby girl and laid it in his arms, and then a few moments later let him into the room where the pale mother lay, he stooped over her and, kissing her fondly, said:

"I never loved you half as well as I do now."

It was a pretty child, with dark blue eyes, and hair in which there was a gleam of gold, and Guy, when asked what he would call her, said:

"Would you object to Margaret?"

Julia knew what he meant, and, like the true, noble woman she was, offered no objection to Guy's choice, knowing well who Margaret had been; and herself first gave the pet name of Daisy to her child, on whom Guy settled the ten thousand dollars sent to him by the Daisy over the sea.

CHAPTER IX

DAISY, TOM, AND THAT OTHER ONE

Watching, waiting, hoping, saying to herself in the morning, "It will come before night," and saying to herself at night, "It will be here to-morrow morning." Such was Daisy's life, even before she had a right to expect an answer to her letter.

Of the nature of Guy's reply she had no doubt. He had loved her once, he loved her still, and he would take her back of course. There was no truth in that rumor of another marriage. Possibly her father, whom she understood now better than she once had, had gotten the story up for the sake of inducing her through pique to marry Tom; but if so his plan would fail. Guy would write to her, "Come!" and she would go, and more than once she counted the contents of her purse and added to it the sum due her from Madame Lafarcade, and wondered if she would dare venture on the journey with so small a sum.

"You so happy and white, too, *ce matin*," her little pupil, Pauline, said to her one day, when they sat together in the garden, and Daisy was indulging in a fanciful picture of her meeting with Guy.

"Yes, I am happy," Daisy said, rousing from her reverie; "but

I did not know I was pale—or white, as you term it—though, now I think of it, I do feel sick and faint. It's the heat, I guess. Oh! there is Max with the mail! He is coming this way! He has—he certainly has something for me!"

Daisy's cheeks were scarlet now, and her eyes were bright as stars as she went forward to meet the man who brought the letters to the house.

"Only a paper!—is there nothing more?" she asked in an unsteady voice, as she took the paper in her hand, and, recognizing Guy's handwriting, knew almost to a certainty what was before her.

"Oh, mon Dieu! vous etes malade! J'apporterai un verre d'eau!" Pauline exclaimed, forgetting her English and adopting her mother tongue in her alarm at Daisy's white face and the peculiar tone of her voice.

"No, Pauline, stay; open the paper for me," Daisy said, feeling that it would be easier so than to read it herself, for she knew it was there, else he would never have sent her a paper and nothing more.

Delighted to be of some use, and a little gratified to open a foreign paper, Pauline tore off the wrapper, starting a little at Daisy's quick, sharp cry as she made a rent across the handwriting.

"Look, you are tearing into my name, which he wrote," Daisy said, and then remembering herself, she sank back into her seat in the garden chair, while Pauline wondered what harm there was in tearing an old soiled wrapper, and why her governess should take it so carefully in her hand and roll it up as if it had been a living thing.

There were notices of new books, and a runaway match in high life, and a suicide on Summer Street, and a golden wedding in Roxbury, and the latest fashions from Paris, into which Pauline plunged with avidity while Daisy listened like one in a dream, asking when the fashions were exhausted: "Is that all? Are there no deaths or marriages?"

Pauline had not thought of that—she would see, and she hunted through the columns till she found Guy's pencil mark, and read:

"Married, this morning, at St. Paul's Church, by the Rev. Dr.—, assisted by the rector, Guy Thornton, Esq., of Cuylerville, to Miss Julia Hamilton, of this city."

"Yes, yes; it's very hot here, isn't it? I think I will go in," Daisy said, her fingers working nervously with the bit of paper she held.

But Pauline was too intent on the name of Thornton to hear what Daisy said, and she asked: "Is Mr. Thornton your friend?"

It was a natural enough question, and Daisy roused herself to answer it, and said quickly: "He is the son of my husband's father."

"Oh, oui," Pauline rejoined, a little mystified as to the exact relationship existing between Guy Thornton and her teacher's husband, whom she supposed was dead, as Daisy had only confided to madame the fact of a divorce.

"What date is the paper?" Daisy asked, and on being told she said softly to herself: "I see, it was too late."

There was in her mind no doubt as to what the result would

Mary J. Holmes

have been had her letter been in time; no doubt of Guy's preference for her; no regret that she had written to him, except that the knowledge that she loved him at last might make him wretched with thinking "what might have been," and with the bitter pain which cut her heart like a knife there was mingled a pity for Guy, who would perhaps suffer more than she did, if that were possible. She never once thought of retribution, or of murmuring against her fate, but accepted it meekly, albeit she staggered under the load and grew faint as she thought of the lonely life before her, and she so young.

Slowly she went back to her room, while Pauline walked up and down the garden trying to make out the relationship between the newly married Thornton and her teacher.

"The son of her husband's father?" she repeated, until at last a meaning dawned upon her, and she said: "Then he must be her brother-in-law; but why didn't she say so? Maybe, though, that is the English way of putting it," and, having thus settled the matter, Pauline joined her mother, who was asking for Mrs. Thornton.

"Gone to her room, and her brother-in-law is married. It was marked in a paper and I read it to her, and she's sick," Pauline said, without, however, in the least connecting the sickness with the marriage.

Daisy did not come down to dinner that night, and the maid who called her the next morning reported her as ill and acting very strangely. Through the summer a malarial fever had prevailed to some extent in and about Rouen, and the physician whom Madame Lafarcade summoned to the sick girl expressed a fear that she was coming down with it, and ordered her kept as quiet as possible.

"She seems to have something weighing on her mind. Has

she heard any bad news from home?" he asked, as in reply to his question where her pain was the worst Daisy always answered:

"It reached him too late—too late, and I am so sorry."

Madame knew of no bad news, she said, and then as she saw the foreign paper lying on the table, she took it up, and, guided by the pencil marks, read the notice of Guy Thornton's marriage, and that gave her the key at once to Daisy's mental agitation. Daisy had been frank with her and told her as much of her story as was necessary, and she knew that the Guy Thornton married to Julia Hamilton had once called Daisy his wife.

"Excuse me, she is, or she has something on her mind, I suspect," she said to the physician, who was still holding Daisy's hand and looking anxiously at her flushed cheeks and bright, restless eyes.

"I thought so," he rejoined, "and it aggravates all the symptoms of her fever. I shall call again to-night."

He did call and found his patient worse, and the next day he asked Madame Lafarcade:

"Has she friends in this country? If so, they ought to know."

A few hours later, and in his lodgings at Berlin, Tom read the following dispatch:

"Mrs. Thornton is dangerously ill. Come at once."

It was directed to Mr. McDonald, who with his wife had been on a trip to Russia, and was expected daily. Feeling intuitively that it concerned Daisy, Tom had opened it, and without a moment's hesitation packed his valise, and, leaving a note for the McDonalds when they should return, started for Rouen. Daisy did not know him, and in her delirium she said things to him and of him which hurt him cruelly. Guy was her theme, and the letter which went "too late, too late." Then she would beg of Tom to go for Guy, to bring him to her and tell him how much she loved him and how good she would be if he would take her back.

"Father wants me to marry Tom," she said in a whisper, and Tom's heart almost stood still as he listened; "and Tom wanted me, too, but I couldn't, you know, even if he were worth his weight in gold. I could not love him. Why, he's got red hair, and such great freckles on his face, and big feet and hands with freckles on them. Do you know Tom?"

"Yes, I know him," Tom answered sadly, forcing down a choking sob, while the "big hand with the great freckles on it" smoothed the golden hair tenderly and pushed it back from the burning brow.

"Don't talk any more, Daisy; it tires you so," he said, as he saw her about to speak again.

But Daisy was not to be stopped, and she went on:

"Tom is good, though; so good, but awkward, and I like him ever so much, but I can't be his wife. I cannot. I cannot."

"He doesn't expect it now, or want it," came huskily from Tom, while Daisy quickly asked:

"Doesn't he?"

"No, never any more; so, put it from your mind and try to sleep," Tom said, and again the freckled hands smoothed the tumbled pillows and wiped the sweat drops from Daisy's face, while all the time the great kind heart was breaking, and the hot tears were rolling down the sun-burned face Daisy thought was so ugly.

Tom had heard from Madame Lafarcade of Guy's marriage, and, like her, understood why Daisy's fever ran so high and her mind was in such a turmoil. But for himself he knew there was no hope, and with a feeling of death in his heart he watched by her day and night, yielding his place to no one, and saying to madame when she remonstrated with him and bade him care for his own health:

"It does not matter to me. I would rather die than not."

Daisy was better when her mother came—saved, the doctor said, more by Tom's care and nursing than by his own skill, and then Tom gave up his post and never went near her unless she asked for him. His "red hair and freckled face" were constantly in his mind, making him loathe the very sight of himself.

"She cannot bear my looks, and I will not force myself upon her," he said; and so he stayed away, but surrounded her with every luxury money could buy, and, as soon as she was able, had her removed to a pretty little cottage which he rented and fitted up for her, and where she would be more at home and quieter than at Madame Lafarcade's.

And there, one morning when he called to inquire for her, he, too, was smitten down with the fever which he had taken with Daisy's breath the many nights and days he watched her without rest or sufficient food. There was a faint, followed by a long interval of unconsciousness, and when he came to himself he was in Daisy's own room, lying on Daisy's little bed, and Daisy herself was bending anxiously over him with a flush on her white cheeks and a soft, pitiful look in her blue eyes.

"What is it? Where am I?" he asked, and Daisy replied:

"You are here in my room—on my bed; and you've got the fever, and I'm going to take care of you, and I'm so glad. Not glad you have the fever," she added, as she met his look of wonder, "but glad I can repay in part all you did for me, you dear, noble Tom! And you are not to talk," and she laid her small hand on his mouth as she saw him about to speak. "I am strong enough; the doctor says so, and I'd do it if he didn't, for you are the best, the truest friend I have."

She was rubbing his hot, feverish hands, and though the touch of her cool, soft fingers was so delicious, poor Tom thought of the big freckles so obnoxious to the little lady, and, drawing his hands from her grasp, hid them beneath the clothes. Gladly, too, would he have covered his face and hair from her sight, but this he could not do and breathe, but he begged her to leave him and send someone in her place. But Daisy would not listen to him.

He had nursed her day and night, she said, and she should stay with him, and she did, through three weeks, when Tom's fever ran higher than hers had done, because there was more for it to feed upon, and when Tom in his ravings talked of things which made her heart ache with a new and different pain from that already there.

At first there were low whisperings and incoherent mutterings, and when Daisy asked him to whom he was talking he answered her:

"To that other one over in the corner. Don't you see him? He is waiting for me till the fever eats me up. There's a lot of me to eat, I'm so big and awkward, overgrown—that's what Daisy said. You know Daisy, don't you? a dainty little creature, with such delicacy of sight and touch! She doesn't like red hair; she said so when we thought the man in the corner was waiting for her, and she doesn't like my freckled face and hands—big hands, she said they were, and yet how they have worked like horses for her! Oh, Daisy! Daisy! I have loved her ever since she was a child, and I drew her to school on my sled and cut her doll's head off to tease her. Take me quick, please, out of her sight, where my freckled face won't offend her."

He was talking now to that other one, the man in the corner, who, like some grim sentinel, stood there day and night, while Daisy kept her tireless watch and Tom talked on and on—never to her—but always to the other one, the man in the corner, whom he begged to take him away.

"Bring out your boat," he would say. "It's time we were off, for the tide is at its height, and the river is running so fast. I thought once it would take Daisy, but it left her, and I am glad. When I am fairly over and there's nothing but my big, freckled hulk left, cover my face and don't let her look at me, though I'll be white then, not red. Oh, Daisy, Daisy, my darling, you hurt me so cruelly!"

Those were terrible days for Daisy, but she never flinched from her post, and stood resolutely between the sick man and that other one in the corner until the latter seemed to waver a little; his shadow was not so black, his presence so all-pervading, and there was hope for Tom. His reason came back at last, and the fever left him, but weak as a child, with no power to move even his poor wasted hands which lay outside the counterpane and seemed to trouble him, for there was a wistful, pleading look in his gray eyes as they went from the hands to Daisy, while his lips whispered faintly, "Cover."

Mary J. Holmes

She understood him, and with a rain of tears spread the sheet over them, and then on her knees beside him, said to him amid her sobs:

"Forgive me, Tom, for what I did when I was crazy. You are not repulsive to me. You are the truest, best, and dearest friend I ever had, and I—I—oh, Tom, I wish I had never been born."

Daisy did not stay by Tom that night. There was no necessity for it, and she was so worn and weary with watching that the physician declared she must have absolute rest or be sick again herself. So she remained away, and in a little room by herself fought the fiercest battle she had ever fought, and on her knees, with tears and bitter cries, asked for help to do right. Not for help to know what was right. She felt sure that she did know that, only the flesh was weak, and there were chords of love still clinging to a past she scarcely dared think of now lest her courage should fail her. Guy was lost to her forever; it was a sin even to think of him as she must think if she thought at all, and so she strove to put him from her—to tear his image from her heart and put another in its place, even Tom, whom she pitied so much, and whom she could make so happy.

"No matter for myself," she said. "No matter what I feel, or how sharp the pain in my heart, if I only keep it there and never let Tom know. I can make him happy, and I will."

There was no wavering after that decision—no regret for the "might have been," but her face was white as snow, and about the pretty mouth there was a quivering of the muscles as if the words were hard to utter when next day she went to Tom, and, sitting down beside him, asked how he was feeling. His eyes brightened a little when he saw her, but there was a look on his face which made Daisy's pulse quicken with a nameless fear, and his voice was very weak as he replied:

"They say I am better; but, Daisy, I know the time is near for me to go. I shall never get well, nor do I wish to, though life is not a gift to be thrown away easily, and on some accounts mine has been a happy one, but the life beyond is better, and I feel sure I am going to it."

"Oh, Tom, Tom, don't talk so! You must not leave me now!" Daisy cried, all her composure giving way as she fell on her knees beside him, and, taking both his hands in hers, wet them with her tears. "Tom," she began, when she could speak. "I have been bad to you so often, and worried and wounded you so much; but I am sorry, so sorry, and I've thought it all over and made up my mind, and I want you to get well and ask me that—that—question again—you have asked so many times—and—and—Tom—I will say—yes—to it now, and try so hard to make you happy."

Her face was crimson as if with shame, and she dared not look at Tom until his silence startled her. Then she stole a glance at his face and met an expression which prompted her to go on recklessly:

"Don't look so incredulous, Tom. I am in earnest. I mean what I say, though it may be unmaidenly to say it. Try me, Tom; I will make you happy, and, though at first I cannot love you as I did Guy when I sent him that letter, the love will come, born of your great goodness and kindness of heart. Try me, Tom, won't you?"

She kissed his thin, white hands where the freckles shone more plainly than ever, and which Tom tried to free from her; she held them fast and looked steadily into the face, which shone for a moment with a joy so great that it was almost handsome, and when she said again, "Will you, Tom?" the pale lips parted with an effort to speak, but no sound was audible, only the chin quivered, and the tears stood in his gray eyes as he battled with the great temptation. Should he accept the sacrifice? Ought he to join her life with his? Could she ever learn to love him? No, she could not, and he must put her from him, even though she came asking him to take her. Thus Tom decided, and, turning his face to the wall, he said, with a choking sob:

"No, Daisy—no. It cannot be. Such happiness is not for me now. I must not think of it. Thank you, darling, just the same. It was kind in you and well meant, but it cannot be. I could not make you happy. I am not like Guy; never can be like him, and you would hate me after a while, and the chain would hurt you cruelly. No, Daisy, I love you too well—and yet, Daisy—Daisy—why do you tempt me so—if it could have been!"

He turned suddenly toward her, and, winding both his arms around her, drew her to him in a quick, passionate embrace, crying piteously over her, and saying:

"My darling, my darling, if it could have been, but it's too late now—God is good and will take me to himself. I thought of it before I was sick, and believe I am a better man, and Jesus is my friend, and I am going to him. I'm glad you told me what you have. It will make my last days happier, and when I am gone you will find that I did well with you."

He put her from him then, for faintness and great exhaustion were stealing over him, and that was the last that ever passed between him and Daisy on the subject which all his life had occupied so much of his thoughts. The fever had left him, it is true, but he seemed to have no vital force or rallying power, and after a few days it was clear even to Daisy that

Tom's life was drawing to a close. "The man in the corner" was there again waiting for his prey, and would not leave this time until he bore with him an immortal soul. And Tom was very happy. He had thought much of death and what lay beyond during those days when Daisy's life hung in the balance, and the result of the much thinking had been a full surrender of himself to God, who did not forsake him when the dark, cold river was closing over him.

Calm and peaceful as the setting of the summer sun was the close of his life, and up to the last he retained his consciousness, with the exception of a few hours, when his mind wandered a little, and he talked to "that other one," whom no one could see but whose presence all felt so vividly.

"It would have been pleasant, and for a minute I was tempted to take her at her word," he said; "but when I remembered my hair and face and hands, and how she liked nothing which was not comely, I would not run the chance of being hated for my repulsive looks. Poor little Daisy! she meant it all right, and I bless her for it, and am glad she said it, but she must not look at me when I'm dead. The freckles she dislikes so much will show plainer then. Don't let her come near, or, if she must, cover me up—cover me up—cover me from her sight."

Thus he talked, and Daisy, who knew what he meant, wept silently by his side, and kept the sheet closely drawn over the hands he was so anxious to have hidden from her view. He knew her at last, and bade her a long farewell, and told her she had been to him the dearest thing in life, and Daisy's arm was round him, supporting him upon the pillow, and Daisy's hand wiped the death moisture from his brow, and Daisy's lips were pressed to his dying face, and her ear caught his last faint whisper:

Mary J. Holmes

"God bless you, darling! I am going home! Good-by!"

"The man in the corner—that other one"—had claimed him, and Daisy put gently from her only the lifeless form which had once been Tom.

They buried him there in France on a sunny slope, where the grass was green and the flowers blossomed in the early spring, and when Mr. McDonald examined his papers he found to his surprise that, with the exception of an annuity to himself and several legacies to different charitable institutions, Tom had left to Daisy his entire fortune, stipulating only that one-tenth of all her income should be yearly given back to God, who had a right to it.

CHAPTER X

MISS MCDONALD

She took that name again, and with it, also, Margaret, feeling that Daisy was far too girlish an appellation for one who clad herself almost in widow's weeds, and felt, when she stood at poor Tom's grave, more wretched and desolate than many a wife has felt when her husband was put from her sight.

Tom had meant to make her parents independent of her so that she need not have them with her unless she chose to do so, for, knowing Mr. McDonald as he did, he thought she would be happier alone, but God so ordered it that within three months after poor Tom's death they made another grave beside his, and Daisy and her mother were alone.

It was spring-time now, and the two desolate women bade adieu to their dead, and made their way to England, and from there to Scotland, where among the heather hills they passed the summer in the utmost seclusion.

Here Daisy had ample time for thought, which dwelt mostly upon the past and the happiness she cast away when she consented to the sundering of the tie which had bound her to Guy Thornton.

Mary J. Holmes

"Oh, how could I have been so foolish and so weak," she said, as, with intense contempt for herself, she read over the journal she had kept at Elmwood during the first weeks of her married life.

Guy had said it would be pleasant for her to refer to its pages in after years, little dreaming with what sore anguish of heart poor Daisy would one day weep over the senseless things recorded there.

"Can it be I was ever that silly little fool?" she said bitterly, as she finished her journal. "And how could Guy love me as I know he did. Oh, if I but had the chance again, I would make him so happy! Oh, Guy, Guy—my husband still—mine more than Julia's, if you could know how much I love you now; nor can I feel it wrong to do so, even though I never hope to see your face again. Guy, Guy, the world is so desolate, and I am young, only twenty-three, and life is so long and dreary with nothing to live for or to do. I wish almost that I were dead like Tom, only I dare not think I should go to heaven where he has gone."

In her sorrow and loneliness Daisy was fast sinking into an unhealthy, morbid state of mind from which nothing seemed to arouse her.

"Nothing to live for—nothing to do," was her lament until one golden September day, when there came a turning point in her life, and she found there was something to do.

There was no regular service that Sunday in the church where she usually attended, and as the day was fine and she was far too restless to remain at home, she proposed to her mother that they walk to a little chapel about a mile away, where a young Presbyterian clergyman was to preach.

She had heard much of his eloquence, and as his name was McDonald, he might possibly be some distant relative. Inasmuch as her father was of Scotch descent she felt a double interest in him, and with her mother was among the first who entered the little, humble building and took a seat upon one of the hard, uncomfortable benches near the pulpit.

The speaker was young—about Tom's age—and with a look on his florid face and a sound in his voice so like that of the dead man that Daisy half started to her feet when he first took his stand in front of her and announced the opening hymn. His text was: "Why stand ye here all the day idle?" and so well did he handle it, and so forcible were his gestures and eloquent his style of delivery, that Daisy listened to him spellbound, her eyes fixed intently upon his glowing face and her ears drinking in every word he uttered.

After dwelling for a time upon the loiterers in God's vineyard, the idlers from choice, who worked not for lack of an inclination to do so, he spoke next of the class whose whole life was a weariness for want of something to do, and to these he said: "Have you never read how, when the disciples rebuked the grateful woman for wasting upon her Master's head what might have been sold for three hundred pence and given to the poor, Jesus said unto them, 'The poor ye have with you always,' and is it not so, my hearers? Are there no poor at your door to be fed, no hungry little ones to be cared for out of the abundance which God has only loaned you for this purpose? Are there no wretched homes which you can make happier, no aching hearts which a kind word would cheer? Remember there is a blessing pronounced for even the cup of cold water, and how much greater shall be the reward of those who, forgetting themselves, seek the good of others and turn not away from the needy and the desolate. See to it, then, you to whom God has given much. See to it that you sit not down in idle ease, wasting upon yourself alone the goods designed for others, for to whom much is given of him much shall be required."

Attracted, perhaps, by the deep black of Daisy's attire, or the something about her which marked her as different from the mass of his hearers, the speaker had seemed to address the last of his remarks directly to her, and had the dead Tom risen from his grave and spoken with her face to face, she could hardly have been more affected than she was. The resemblance was so striking and the voice so like her cousin's that she felt as if she had received a message direct from him; or, if not from him, she surely had from God, whose almoner she henceforth would be.

That day was the beginning of a new life to her. Thenceforth there must be no more repining; no more idle, listless days, no more wishing for something to do. There was work all around her, and she found it and did it with a will—first, from a sense of duty, and at last for the real pleasure it afforded her to carry joy and gladness to the homes where want and sorrow had sat so long.

Hearing that there were sickness and destitution among the miners in Peru, where her possessions were, she went early in November, and many a wretched heart rejoiced because of her, and many a lip blessed the beautiful lady whose coming among them was productive of so much good. Better dwellings, better wages, a church, a schoolhouse followed in her footsteps, and then, when everything there seemed in good working order, there came over her a longing for her native country, and the next autumn found her in New York, where in a short space of time everybody knew of the beautiful Miss McDonald, who was a millionaire and who owned the fine house and grounds in the upper part of the city not far from the Park.

Here society claimed her again, and Daisy, who had no morbid fancies now, yielded in part to its claims and became, if not a belle, a favorite, whose praises were in every mouth. But chiefly was she known and loved by the poor and the despised whom she daily visited, and to whom her presence was like the presence of an angel.

"You do look lovely and sing so sweet; I know there's nothing nicer in heaven," said a little piece of deformity to her one day as it lay dying in her arms. "I'se goin' to heaven, which I shouldn't have done if you'se hadn't gin me the nice bun and told me of Jesus. I loves him now, and I'll tell him how you bringed me to him."

Such was the testimony of one dying child, and it was dearer to Daisy than all the words of flattery ever poured into her ear. As she had brought that little child to God, so she would bring others, and she made her work among the children especially, finding there her best encouragement and greatest success.

Once when Guy Thornton chanced to be in the city and driving in the Park, he saw a singular sight—a pair of splendid bays arching their graceful necks proudly, their silver-tipped harness flashing in the sunlight, and their beautiful mistress radiant with happiness as she sat in her large open carriage, not in the midst of gayly dressed friends, but amid a group of poorly clad, pale-faced little ones, to whom the Park was a paradise, and she was the presiding angel.

"Look—that's Miss McDonald," Guy's friend said to him, "the greatest heiress in New York, and I reckon the one who does the most good. Why, she supports more old people and children and runs more ragged schools than any half-dozen men in the city, and I don't suppose there's a den in New York where she has not been, and never once, I'm told, was she insulted, for the vilest of them stand between her and harm. Once a miscreant on Avenue A knocked a boy down for accidentally stepping in a pool of water and sprinkling her white dress in passing. Friday nights she has a reception for these people, and you ought to see how well they behave. At first they were noisy and rough, and she had to have the police, but now they are quiet and orderly as you please. Perhaps you'd like to go to one. I know Miss McDonald, and will take you with me."

Guy said he should not be in town on Friday, as he must return to Cuylerville the next day, and with a feeling he could not quite analyze, he turned to look at the turnout which always excited so much attention. But it was not so much at the handsome bays and the bevy of queer-looking children he gazed as at the little lady in their midst, clad in velvet and ermine, with a long white feather falling among the curls of her bright hair. When Daisy first entered upon her new life she had affected a nun-like garb as one most appropriate, but after a little child said to her once, "I'se don't like your black gown all the time. I likes sumptin' bright and pretty," she changed her mind and gave freer scope to her natural good taste and love of what was becoming. And the result showed the wisdom of the change, for the children and inmates of the dens she visited, accustomed only to the squalor and ugliness of their surroundings, hailed her more rapturously than they had done before, and were never weary of talking of the beautiful woman who was not afraid to wear her pretty clothes into their wretched houses, which, lest she should soil and defile them, gradually grew more clean and tidy for her sake.

"It wasn't for the likes of them gownds to trail through sich truck," Bridget O'Donohue said, and so, on the days when Daisy was expected, she scrubbed the floor, which, until Daisy's advent had not known water for years, and rubbed and polished the one wooden chair kept sacred for the lady's use.

Other women, too, caught Biddy's spirit and scrubbed their floors and their children's faces on the day when Miss McDonald was expected to call, and when she came her silk dress and pretty shawl were watched narrowly lest by some chance a speck of dirt should fasten on them, and her becoming dress and handsome face were commented on and remembered as some fine show which had been seen for nothing. Especially did the children like her in her bright dress, and the velvet and ermine in which she was clad when Guy met her in the Park were worn more for their sakes than for the gaze of those to whom such things were no novelties. To Guy she looked more beautiful than he had ever seen her before, and there was in his heart a smothered feeling as of a want of something lost, as her carriage disappeared from view and he lost sight of the fair face and form which had once been his own.

The world was going well with Guy, for though Dick Trevylian had paid no part of the hundred thousand dollars, and he still lived in the brown cottage on the hill, he was steadily working his way to competency, if not to wealth. His profession as a lawyer, which he had resumed, yielded him a remunerative income, while his contributions to different magazines were much sought after, so that to all human appearance he was prosperous and happy. Prosperous in his business, and happy in his wife and little ones, for there was now a second child, a baby Guy of six weeks old, and when on his return from New York the father bent over the cradle of his boy and kissed his baby face, that image seen in the Park seemed to fade away, and the caresses he gave to Julia had in them no faithlessness or insincerity. She was a noble woman, and had made him a good wife, and he loved her truly, though with a different, less absorbing, less ecstatic love than he had given to Daisy. But he did not tell her of Miss McDonald. Indeed, that name was never spoken now, nor was any reference ever made to her except when little Daisy asked where was the lady for whom she was named, and why she did not send her a doll.

"I hardly think she knows there is such a chit as you," Guy said to her once, when sorely pressed on the subject, and then the child wondered how that could be, and wished she was big enough to write her a letter and ask her to come and see her.

Every day after that little Daisy played "make b'lieve Miss McDolly" was there, said McDolly being represented by a bundle of shawls tied up to look like a figure and seated in a chair. At last there came to the cottage a friend of Julia's, a young lady from New York, who knew Daisy, and who, while visiting in Cuylerville, accidentally learned that she was the divorced wife of whose existence she knew, but of whom she had never spoken to Mrs. Thornton. Hearing the little one talking one day to Miss McDolly and asking her why she never wrote nor sent a "sing" to her sake-name, the young lady said:

"Why don't you send Miss McDonald a letter? You tell me what to say and I'll write it down for you, but don't let mamma know till you see if you get anything."

The little girl's fancy was caught at once with the idea, and the following letter was the result:

"BROWN COTTAGE, 'Most Tissmas time.

"DEAR MISS MCDOLLY:—I'se an 'ittle dirl named for you, I is, Daisy Thornton, an' my papa is Mr. Guy, an' mamma is Julia, and 'ittle brother is Guy, too—only he's a baby, and vomits up his dinner and ties awfully sometimes; an' I knows anoder 'ittle girl named for somebody who dives her 'sings,' a whole lot, an' why doesn't youse dive me some, when I'se your sake-name, an' loves you ever so much, and why'se you never turn here to see me. I wish you would. I ask papa is you pretty, an' he tell me yes, bootiful, an' every night I p'ays for you and say God bress papa an' mam-ma, an' auntie, and Miss McDolly, and 'ittle brodder, an' make Daisy a dood dirl, and have Miss McDolly send her sumptin' for Tissmas, for Christ's sake. An' I wants a turly headed doll that ties and suts her eyes when she does to seep, and wears a shash and a pairesol, and anodder bigger dolly to be her mam-ma and pank her when she's naughty, an' I wants an 'ittle fat-iron, an' a cookstove, an' wash-board. I'se dot a tub. An' I wants some dishes an' a stenshun table, an' 'ittle bedstead, an' yuffled seets, an' pillars, an' blue silk kilt, an' ever so many sings which papa cannot buy, 'cause he hasn't dot the money. Vill you send them, Miss McDolly, pese, an' your likeness, too. I wants to see how you looks. My mam-ma is pretty, with black hair an' eyes, but she's awful old—I dess. How old is you? Papa's hair is some dray, an' his viskers, too. My eyes is bue.

"Yours respectfully, DAISY THORNTON."

*　*　*　*　*

Miss McDonald had been shopping since ten in the morning, and her carriage had stood before the dry-goods stores, and toy-shops, and candy stores, while bundle after bundle had been deposited on the cushions, and others ordered to be sent. But she was nearly through now, and just as it was beginning to grow dark in the streets she bade her coachman drive home, where dinner was waiting for her in the dining room, and her mother was waiting in the parlor. Mrs. McDonald was not very well, and had kept her room all day,

Mary J. Holmes

but she was better that night, and came down to dine with her daughter. The December wind was cold and raw, and a few snowflakes fell on Daisy's hat and cloak as she ran up the steps and entered the warm, bright room, which seemed so pleasant when contrasted with the dreariness without.

"Oh, how nice this is, and how tired and cold I am!" she said, as she bent over the blazing fire.

"Are you through with your shopping?" Mrs. McDonald asked, in a half-querulous tone, as if she did not altogether approve of her daughter's acts.

"Yes, all through, except a shawl for old Sarah Mackie and a few more toys for Biddy Warren's blind boy," Daisy said, and her mother replied: "Well, I'm sure I shall be glad for your sake when it is over. You'll make yourself sick, and you are nearly worn out now, remembering everybody in New York."

"Not quite everybody, mother," Daisy rejoined cheerfully; "only those whom everybody forgets—the poor, whom we have with us always. Don't you remember the text and the little kirk where we heard it preached from? But come— dinner is ready, and I am hungry, I assure you."

She led the way to the handsome dining room, and took her seat at the table, looking, in her dark street dress, as her mother had said, pale and worn, as if the shopping had been very hard upon her. And yet it was not so much the fatigue of the day which affected her as the remembrance of a past she did not often dare to recall.

It was at Christmas time years ago that she first met with Guy, and all the day long, as she turned over piles of shawls and delaines and flannels, or ordered packages of candy and bonbons and dollies by the dozen, her thoughts had been with Guy and the time she met him at Leiter and Field's and he walked home with her. It seemed to her years and years ago, and the idea of having lived so long made her feel old, and tired, and worn. But the nice dinner and the cheer of the room revived her, and her face looked brighter and more rested when she returned to the parlor and began to show her mother her purchases.

Daisy did not receive many letters except on business, and as these usually came in the morning she did not think to ask if the postman had left her anything; and so it was not until her mother had retired and she was about going to her own room that she saw a letter lying on the hall-stand. Miss Barker, who had instigated the letter, had never written to her more than once or twice, and then only short notes, and she did not recognize the handwriting at once. But she saw it was postmarked Cuylerville, and a sick, faint sensation crept over her as she wondered who had sent it, and if it contained news of Guy. It was long since she had heard of him—not, in fact, since poor Tom's death, and she knew nothing of the little girl called for herself, and thus had no suspicion of the terrible shock awaiting her, when at last she broke the seal. Miss Barker had written a few explanatory lines, which were as follows:

"CUYLERVILLE, Dec., 18—

"DEAR MISS MCDONALD—Since saying good-by to you last June, and going off to the mountains and seaside, while you like a good Samaritan stayed in the hot city to look after 'your people,' I have flitted hither and thither until at last I floated out to Cuylerville to visit Mrs. Guy Thornton, who is a friend and former schoolmate of mine. Here—not in the house, but in town—I have heard a story which surprised me not a little, and I now better understand that sad look I have so often seen on your sweet face without at all suspecting the cause.

"Dear friend, pardon me, won't you, for the liberty I have taken since knowing your secret? You would, I am sure, if you only knew what a dear, darling little creature Mr. Thornton's eldest child is. Did you know he had called her Daisy for you? He has, and with her blue eyes and bright auburn hair, she might pass for your very own, with the exception of her nose, which is decidedly retrousse. She is three years old, and the most precocious little witch you ever saw. What think you of her making up a bundle of shawls and aprons and christening it Miss McDolly, her name for you, and talking to it as if it were really the famous and beautiful woman she fancies it to be? She is your 'sake-name,' she says, and before I knew the facts of the case, I was greatly amused by her talk to the bundle of shawls which she reproached for never having sent her anything. When I asked Julia (that's Mrs. Thornton) who Miss McDolly was, she merely answered, 'The lady for whom Daisy was named,' and that was all I knew until the gossips enlightened me, when, without a word to anyone, I resolved upon a liberty which I thought I could venture to take with you. I suggested the letter which I inclose and which I wrote exactly as the words came from the little lady's lips. Neither Mr. Thornton nor his wife know aught of the letter, nor will they unless you respond, for the child will keep her own counsel, I am well assured.

"Again forgive me if I have done wrong, and believe me, as ever,

"Yours, sincerely, "ELLA BARKER."

Daisy's face was as pale as ashes as she read Miss Barker's letter, and then snatching up the other, devoured its contents almost at a glance, while her breath came in panting gasps and her heart seemed trying to burst through her throat. She could neither move nor cry out for a moment, but she sat like one turned into stone with that sense of suffocation oppressing her, and that horrible pain in her heart. She had thought the grave was closed, the old wound healed by time and silence; and now a little child had torn it open, and it was bleeding and throbbing again with a pang such as she had never felt before, while there crept over her such a feeling of desolation and loneliness, a want of something unpossessed, as few have ever experienced.

But for her own foolishness that sweet little child might have been hers, she thought, as her heart went after the little one with an indescribable yearning which made her stretch out her arms as if to take the baby to her bosom and hold it there forever. Guy had called it for her, and that touched her more than anything else. He had not forgotten her then. She had never supposed he had, but to be thus assured of it was very sweet, and as she thought of it and read again little Daisy's letter, the tightness about her heart and the choking sensation in her throat began to give way, and one after another the great tears rolled down her cheeks, slowly at first, but gradually faster and faster, until they fell in torrents and a tempest of sobs shook her slight frame as with her head bowed upon her dressing-table she gave vent to her grief. It seemed to her she never could stop crying or grow calm again, for as often as she thought of the touching words, "I p'ays for you," there came a fresh burst of sobs and tears, until at last nature was exhausted, and with a low moan Daisy sank upon her knees and tried to pray, the words which first sprang to her lips framing themselves into thanks that somewhere in the world there was one who prayed for her and loved her, too, even though the love might have for its object merely dolls and candies and toys. And these the child should have in such abundance, and Miss McDonald found herself longing for the morrow in which to begin again the shopping she had thought was nearly ended.

It was in vain next day that her mother remonstrated against her going out, pleading her white, haggard face and the rawness of the day. Daisy was not to be detained at home, and before ten o'clock she was down on Broadway, and the dolly with the "shash" and "pairesol" which she had seen the day before under its glass case was hers for twenty-five dollars, and the plainer bit of china, who was to be dollie's mother and perform the parental duty of "panking her when she was naughty," was also purchased, and the dishes and the table and stove and bedstead, with ruffled sheets and pillow-cases and blue satin spread and the washboard and clothes bars and tiny wringer, with divers others toys, were bought with a disregard of expense which made Miss McDonald a wonder to those who waited on her. Such a Christmas box was seldom sent to a child as that which Daisy packed in her room that night, with her mother looking on and wondering what Sunday-school was to be the recipient of all those costly presents and suggesting that cheaper articles would have answered just as well.

Everything the child had asked for was there except the picture. That Daisy dared not send, lest it should look too much like thrusting herself upon Guy's notice and wound Julia, his wife.

Daisy was strangely pitiful in her thoughts of Julia, who would in her turn have pitied her for her delusion could she have known how sure she was that but for the tardiness of that letter Guy would have chosen his first love in preference to any other.

And it was well that each believed herself first in the affection of the man to whom Daisy wanted so much to send something as a proof of her unalterable love. They were living still in the brown cottage; they were not able to buy Elmwood back. Oh, if she only dared to do it, and could do it, how gladly her Christmas gift should be the handsome place which they had been so proud of! But that would hardly do; Guy might not like to be so much indebted to her; he was proud and sensitive in many points, and so she abandoned the plan for the present, thinking that by and by she would purchase and hold it as a gift to her namesake on her bridal day. That will be better, she said, as she put the last article in the box and saw it leave the door, directed to Guy Thornton's care.

*   *   *   *   *

Great was the surprise at the brown cottage, when, on the very night before Christmas, the box arrived and was deposited in the dining room, where Guy and Julia, Miss Barker and Daisy gathered eagerly around it, the latter exclaiming:

"I knows where it tum from, I do. My sake-name, Miss McDolly, send it, see did. I writ and ask her would see an' she hab."

"What!" Guy said, as, man-like, he began deliberately to untie every knot in the string which his wife in her impatience would have cut at once. "What does the child mean? Do you know, Julia?"

"I do. I'll explain," Miss Barker said, and in as few words as possible she told what she had done, while Julia listened with a very grave face, and Guy was pale even to his lips as he went on untying the string and opening the box.

There was a letter lying on the top which he handed to Julia, who steadied her voice to read aloud:

"NEW YORK, December 22, 18—

"DARLING LITTLE SAKE-NAME DAISY: Your letter made Miss McDolly very happy, and she is so glad to send you the doll with a shash, and the other toys. Write to me again and tell me if they suit you. God bless you, sweet little one, is the prayer of

"MISS MCDONALD."

After that the grave look left Julia's face, and Guy was not quite so pale, as he took out one after another the articles which little Daisy hailed with rapturous shouts and exclamations of delight.

"Oh, isn't she dood, and don't you love her, papa?" she said, while Guy replied:

"Yes, it was certainly very kind in her, and generous. No other little girl in town will have such a box as this."

He was very pale, and there was a strange look in his eyes, but his voice was perfectly natural as he spoke, and one who knew nothing of his former relations to Miss McDonald would never have suspected how his whole soul was moved by this gift to his little daughter.

"You must write and thank her," he said to Julia, who, knowing that this was proper, assented without a word, and when on the morning after Christmas Miss McDonald opened with trembling hands the envelope bearing the Cuylerville postmark, she felt a keen pang of disappointment in finding only a few lines from Julia expressive of her own and little Daisy's thanks for the beautiful Christmas box, "which made our little girl so happy."

Not Julia, but Mrs. Guy, and that hurt Daisy more than anything else.

"Mrs. Guy Thornton! Why need she thrust upon me the name I used to bear?" she whispered, and her lip quivered a little, and the tears sprang to her eyes as she remembered all that lay between the present and the time when she had been Mrs. Guy Thornton.

She was Miss McDonald now, and Guy was another woman's husband, and with a bitter pain in her heart, she put away Julia's letter, saying as she did so, "And that's the end of that."

The box business had not resulted just as she hoped it would. She had thought Guy would write himself, and by some word or allusion assure her of his remembrance, but instead there had come to her a few perfectly polite and well-expressed lines from Julia, who had the impertinence to sign herself Mrs. Guy Thornton! It was rather hard and sorely disappointing, and for many days Miss McDonald's face was very white and sad, and both the old and young whom she visited as usual wondered what had come over the beautiful lady to make her "so pale and sorry."

CHAPTER XI

AT SARATOGA

There were no more letters from Mrs. Guy Thornton until the next Christmas time, when another box went to little Daisy, and was acknowledged as before. Then another year glided by, with a third box to Daisy, and then one summer afternoon in August there came to Saratoga a gay party from New York, and the clerk at Congress Hall registered, with other names, that of Miss McDonald. Indeed, it seemed to be her party, or at least she was its center, and the one to whom the others deferred as to their head. Daisy was in perfect health that summer, and in unusually good spirits, and when in the evening, yielding to the entreaties of her friends, she entered the ball-room, clad in flowing, gauzy robes of blue and white, with costly jewels on her neck and arms, she took all hearts by storm, and was acknowledged at once as the star and belle of the evening. She did not dance—she rarely did that now—but after a short promenade through the room she took a seat near the door, and was watching the gay dancers when she felt her arm softly touched, and, turning, saw her maid standing by her with an anxious, frightened look upon her face.

"Come, please, come quick," she said in a whisper, and, following her out, Miss McDonald asked what was the matter.

"This—you must go away at once. I'll pack your things. I promised not to tell, but I must. I can't see your pretty face all spoiled and ugly."

"What do you mean?" the lady asked, and after a little she made out from the girl's statement that in strolling on the back piazza she had stumbled upon her first cousin, of whose whereabouts she had known nothing for a long time.

The girl, Mary, had, it seemed, come to Saratoga a week or ten days before, with her master's family, consisting of his wife and two children. As the hotel was crowded they were assigned rooms for the night in a distant part of the house, with a promise of something much better on the morrow. In the morning, however, the lady, who had not been well for some days, was too sick to leave her bed, and the doctor who was called in to see her, pronounced the disease—here Sarah stopped and gasped for breath and looked behind her and all ways, and finally whispered a word which made even Miss McDonald start a little and wince with fear.

"He do call it the very-o-lord," Sarah said, "but Mary says it's the very old devil himself. She knows, she has had it, and you can't put down a pin where the cratur didn't have his claws. They told the landlord, who was fur puttin' 'em straight outdoors, but the doctor said the lady must not be moved—it was sure death to do it. It was better to keep quiet, and not make a panic. Nobody need to know it in the house, and their rooms are so far from everybody that nobody would catch it. So he let 'em stay, and the gentleman takes care of her, and Mary keeps the children in the next room, and carries and brings the things, and keeps away from everybody. Two of the servants know it, and they've had it, and don't tell, and she said I mustn't, nor come that

Mary J. Holmes

side of the house, but I must tell you so that you can leave to-morrow. The lady is very bad, and nobody takes care of her but Mr. Thornton. Mary takes things to the door, and leaves them outside where he can get them."

"What did you call the gentleman?" Miss McDonald asked, her voice faltering and her cheek blanching a little.

"Mr. Thornton, from Cuylerville, a place far in the country," was the girl's reply, and then, without waiting to hear more, Miss McDonald darted away, and, going to the office, turned the leaves of the register to the date of ten or eleven days ago, and read with a beating heart and quick coming breath:

"Guy Thornton, lady, two children, and servant. Nos.— and —."

Yes, it was Guy; there could be no mistake, and in an instant her resolution was taken. Calling to her maid, she sent for her shawl and hat, and then bidding her follow, walked away in the moonlight. The previous summer when at Saratoga she had received medical treatment from Dr. Schwartz, whom she knew well and to whose office she directed her steps. He seemed surprised to see her at that hour, but greeted her cordially and asked when she came to town and what he could do for her.

"Tell me if this is still a safeguard," she said, baring her beautiful white arm and showing a large round scar. "Will this insure me against disease?"

The doctor's face flushed, and he looked uneasily at her as he took her arm in his hand, and, examining the scar closely, said:

"The points are still distinct. I should say the vaccination was thorough."

"But another will be safer. Have you fresh vaccine?" Daisy asked; and he replied:

"Yes, some just from a young, healthy heifer. I never use the adulterated stuff which has been humanized. How do I know what humors may be lurking in the blood? Why, some of the fairest, sweetest babies are full of scrofula!"

He was going on further with his discussion, when Daisy, who knew his peculiarities, interrupted him:

"Never mind the lecture now. Vaccinate me quick and let me go."

It was soon done, the doctor saying as he put away his vial:

"You were safe without it, I think, and with it you may have no fears whatever."

He looked at her curiously again as if asking what she knew or feared, and, observing the look, Daisy said to him:

"Do you attend the lady at the hotel?"

He bowed affirmatively and glanced uneasily at Sarah, who was looking on in surprise.

"Is she very sick?" was the next inquiry.

"Yes, very sick."

"And does no one care for her but her husband?"

"No one."

"Has she suffered for care—a woman's care, I mean?"

"Well, not exactly, and yet she might be more comfortable with a woman about her. Women are naturally better nurses than men, and Mr. Thornton is quite worn out, but it does not make much difference now; the lady—"

Daisy did not hear the last part of the sentence, and, bidding him good-night, she went back to the hotel as swiftly as she had left it, while the doctor stood watching the flutter of her white dress, wondering how she found it out, and if she would "tell and raise thunder generally."

"Of course not. I know her better than that," he said to himself. "Poor woman [referring then to Julia], nothing, I fear, can help her now."

Meanwhile Daisy reached the hotel, and without going to her own room, bade Sarah tell her the way to No.—.

"What! Oh, Miss McDonald! You surely are not—" Sarah gasped, clutching at the dress, which her mistress took from her grasp, saying:

"Yes, I am going to see that lady. I know her, or of her, and I'm not afraid. Must we let her die alone?"

"But your face—your beautiful face," Sarah said, and then Daisy did hesitate a moment, and, glancing into a hall mirror, wondered how the face she saw there, and which she knew was beautiful, would look scarred and disfigured as she had seen faces in New York.

There was a momentary conflict, and then, with an inward

prayer that Heaven would protect her, she passed on down the narrow hall and knocked softly at No.——, while Sarah stood wringing her hands in genuine distress, and feeling as if her young mistress had gone to certain ruin.

CHAPTER XII

IN THE SICK-ROOM

Julia had the smallpox, not varioloid, but the veritable thing itself, in its most aggravated form. Where she took it, or when, she did not know, nor did it matter. She had it, and for ten days she had seen no one but her husband and physician, and had no care but such as Guy could give her. He had been unremitting in his attention. Tender and gentle as a woman, he had nursed her night and day, with no thought for himself and the risk he ran. It was a bad disease at the best, and now in its worst type it was horrible, but Julia bore up bravely, thinking always more of others than of herself, and feeling so glad that Providence had sent them to those out-of-the-way rooms, where she had at first thought she could not pass a night comfortably. Her children were in the room adjoining, and she could hear their little voices as they played together, or asked for their mamma and why they must not see her. Alas! they would never see her again; she knew it now, and Guy knew it, too. The doctor had told them so when he left them that night, and between the husband and wife words had been spoken such as are only said when hearts which have been one are about to be severed forever.

To Julia there was no terror in death, save as it took her from those she loved, her husband and her little ones, and these she had given into God's keeping, knowing his promises are sure. To Guy she had said:

"You have made me so happy. I want you to remember that when I am gone; I would not have one look or act of yours changed if I could, and yet, forgive me, Guy, for saying it, but I know you must often have thought of that other one whom, you loved first, and it may be best."

Guy could not say no to that, but he smoothed her hair tenderly, and his tears dropped upon the scarred, swollen face he could not kiss, as Julia went on.

"But if you did you never showed it in the least, and I bless you for it. Take good care of my children; teach them to remember their mother, and if in time there comes another in my place, and other little ones than mine call you father, don't forget me quite, because I love you so much. Oh, Guy, my darling, it is hard to say good-by and know that after a little this world will go on the same as if I had never been. Don't think I am afraid. I am not, for Jesus is with me, and I know I am safe, but still there's a clinging to life, which has been so pleasant to me. Tell your sister how I loved her. I know she will miss me and be good to my children, and if you ever meet that other one tell her—tell her—I—"

The faint voice faltered here, and when it spoke again, it said:

"Lift me up, Guy, so I can breathe better while I tell you."

He lifted her up and held her in his arms, while through the open window the summer air and the silver moonlight streamed, and in the distance was heard the sound of music as the dance went merrily on. And just then, when she was in the minds of both, Daisy came, and her gentle knock broke the silence of the room and startled both Guy and Julia.

Who was it that sought entrance to that death-laden and disease-poisoned room? Not the doctor, surely, for he always entered unannounced, and who else dared to come there? Thus Guy questioned, hesitating to answer the knock, when to his utter surprise the door opened and a little figure, clad in airy robes of white, with its bright hair wreathed with flowers and gems, came floating in, the blue eyes shining like stars and the full red lips parted with the smile, half pleased, half shy, which Guy remembered so well.

"Daisy, Daisy!" he cried, and his voice rang like a bell through the room, as, laying Julia's head back upon the pillow, he sprang to Daisy's side, and, taking her by the shoulder, pushed her gently toward the door, saying:

"Why have you come here? Leave us at once; don't you see? don't you know?" and he pointed toward Julia, whose face showed so plainly in the gaslight.

"Yes, I know, and I came to help you take care of her. I am not afraid," Daisy said, and, freeing herself from his grasp, she walked straight up to Julia and laid her soft, white hand upon her head. "I am Daisy," she said, "and I've come to take care of you. I just heard you were here; how hot your poor head is! let me bathe it; shall I?"

She went to the bowl, and wringing a cloth in ice water, bathed and rubbed the sick woman's head, and held the cool cloth to the face and wiped the parched lips, and rubbed the feverish hands, while Guy stood, looking on, bewildered and confounded, and utterly unable to say a word or utter a protest to this angel, as it seemed to him, who had come unbidden to his aid, forgetful of the risk she ran and the danger she incurred. Once as she turned her beautiful face to him and he saw how wondrously fair and lovely it was, lovely with a different expression from any he had ever seen there, it came over him with a thrill of horror that that face must not be marred and disfigured with the terrible pestilence, and he made another effort to send her away. But Daisy would not go.

"I am not afraid," she said. "I have just been vaccinated, and there was already a good scar on my arm; look!" and she pushed back her sleeve and showed her round, white arm with the mark upon it.

Guy did not oppose her after that, but let her do what she liked, and when, an hour later, the doctor came he found his recent visitor sitting on Julia's bed, with Julia's head lying against her bosom and Julia herself asleep. Some word which sounded very much like "thunderation" escaped his lips, but he said no more, for he saw in the sleeping woman's face a look he never mistook. It was death, and ten minutes after he entered the room Julia Thornton lay dead in Daisy's arms.

There was a moment or so of half-consciousness, during which they caught the words. "So kind in you; it makes me easier; be good to the children; one is called for you, but Guy loved me, too. Good-by. I am going to Jesus."

That was the last she ever spoke, and a moment after she was gone. In his fear lest the facts should be known to his guests, the host insisted that the body should be removed under cover of the night, and as Guy knew the railway officials would object to taking it on any train, there was no alternative except to bury it in town, and so before the morning broke there was brought up to the room a closely sealed coffin and box, and Daisy helped lay Julia in her last bed, and put a white flower in her hair and folded her hands

Mary J. Holmes

upon her bosom, and then watched from the window the little procession which followed the body out to the cemetery, where, in the stillness of the coming day, they buried it, together with everything which had been used about the bed, Daisy's party dress included; and when at last the full morning broke, with stir and life in the hotel, all was empty and still in the fumigated chamber of death, and in the adjoining room, clad in a simple white wrapper, with a blue ribbon in her hair, Daisy sat with Guy's little boy on her lap and her namesake at her side, amusing them as best she could and telling them their mamma had gone to live with Jesus.

"Who'll be our mamma now? We must have one. Will oo?" little Daisy asked, as she hung about the neck of her new friend.

She knew it was Miss McDolly, her "sake-name," and in her delight at seeing her and her admiration of her great beauty, she forgot in part the dead mamma on whose grave the summer sun was shining.

The Thorntons left the hotel that day and went back to the house in Cuylerville, which had been closed for a few weeks, Miss Frances being away with some friends in Connecticut. But she returned at once when she heard the dreadful news, and was there to receive her brother and his motherless little ones. He told her of Daisy when he could trust himself to talk at all, of Julia's sickness and death, and Miss Frances felt her heart go out as it had never gone before toward the woman about whom little Daisy talked constantly.

"Most bootiful lady," she said, "an' looked des like an 'ittle dirl, see was so short, an' her eyes were so hue an' her hair so turly."

Miss McDonald had won Daisy's heart, and, knowing that made her own happier and lighter than it had been since the day when the paper came to her with the marked paragraph which crushed her so completely. There had been but a few words spoken between herself and Guy, and these in the presence of others, but at their parting he had taken her soft little hand in his and held it a moment, while he said, with a choking voice: "God bless you, Daisy. I shall not forget your kindness to my poor Julia, and if you should need—but no, that is too horrible to think of; may God spare you that. Good-by."

And that was all that passed between him and Daisy with regard to the haunting dread which sent her in a few days to her own house in New York, where, if the thing she feared came upon her, she would at least be at home and know she was not endangering the lives of others. But God was good to her, and though there was a slight fever, with darting pains in her back and a film before her eyes, it amounted to nothing worse, and might have been the result of fatigue and over-excitement; and when at Christmas time, yielding to the importunities of her little namesake, there was a picture of herself in the box sent to Cuylerville, the face which Guy scanned even more eagerly than his daughter, was as smooth and fair and beautiful as when he saw it at Saratoga, bending over his dying wife.

Mary J. Holmes

CHAPTER XIII

DAISY'S JOURNAL

NEW YORK, June 14, 18—

To-morrow I am to take my old name of Thornton again, and be Guy's wife once more. Nor does it seem strange at all that I should do so, for I have never thought of myself as not belonging to him, even when I knew he was another's. And yet when in that dreadful night at Saratoga I went to Julia's room, there was in my heart no thought of this which has come to me. I only wished to care for her and to be a help to Guy. I did not think of her dying, and after she was dead there was not a thought of the future in my mind until little Daisy put it there by asking if I would be her mamma. Then I seemed to see it all, and expected it up to the very day, six weeks ago, when Guy wrote to me: "Daisy, I want you. Will you come to me again as my wife?"

I was not surprised. I knew he would say it some time, and I replied at once, "Yes, Guy, I will."

He has been here since, and we have talked it over; all the past when I made him so unhappy, and when I, too, was so wretched, though I did not say much about that, or tell him of the dull, heavy, gnawing pain which, sleeping or waking, I carried with me so long, and only lost when I began to live for others. I did speak of the letter, and said I had loved him ever since I wrote it, and that his marrying Julia made no difference; and when I told him of poor Tom, and what I said to him, not from love, but from a sense of duty, and when I told him how Tom would not take me at my word, he held me close to him and said: "I am glad he did not, my darling, for then you would never have been mine."

I think we both wept over those two graves, one far off in sunny France, the other in Saratoga, and both felt how sad it was that they must be made in order to bring us together. Poor Julia! She was a noble woman, and Guy did love her. He told me so, and I am glad he did. I mean to try to be like her in those parts wherein she excelled me.

We are going straight to Cuylerville to the house where I never was but once, and that on the night when Guy was sick and Miss Frances made me go back in the thunder and rain. She is sorry for that, for she told me so in the long, kind letter she wrote, calling me her little sister and telling me how glad she is to have me back once more. Accidentally I heard Elmwood was for sale, and without letting Guy know I bought it, and sent him the deed, and we are going to make it the most attractive place in the country.

It will be our summer home, but in the winter my place is here in New York with my people, who would starve and freeze without me. Guy has agreed to that and will be a great help to me. He need never work any more unless he chooses to do so, for my agent, says I am a millionaire, thanks to poor Tom, who gave me his gold mine and his interest in that railroad. And for Guy's sake I am glad, and for his children, the precious darlings; how much I love them already, and how kind I mean to be to them both for Julia's sake and Guy's! Hush! That's his ring, and there's his voice in the hall asking for Miss McDonald, and so for the last time I write that name, and sign myself,

MARGARET MCDONALD.

Extracts from Miss Frances Thornton's Diary.

ELMWOOD, June 15,—

I have been looking over an old journal, finished and laid away long ago, and accidentally I stumbled upon a date eleven years back. It was Guy's wedding day then; it is his anniversary now, and as on that June day of years ago I worked among my flowers, so I have been with them this morning, and as then, people from the town came into our beautiful grounds, so they came to-day and praised our lovely place and said there was no place like it in all the country round. But Julia was not with them. She will never come to us again. Julia is dead, and her grave is off in Saratoga, for Guy dare not have her moved, but he has erected a costly monument to her memory, and the mound above her is like some bright flower bed all the summer long, for he hires a man to tend it, and goes twice each season to see that it is kept as he wishes to have it. Julia is in Heaven and Daisy is here again at Elmwood, which she purchased with her own money and fitted up with every possible convenience and luxury.

Guy is ten years younger than he used to be, and we are all so happy with this little fairy, who has expanded into a noble woman, and whom I love as I never loved a living being before, Guy excepted, of course. I never dreamed when I turned her out into the rain that I should love her as I do, or that she was capable of being what she is. I would not have her changed in any one particular, and neither, I am sure, would Guy, while the little ones fairly worship her, and must sometimes be troublesome with their love and their caresses.

It is just a year since she came back to us again. We were in the old house then, but somehow Daisy's very presence seemed to brighten and beautify it, until I was almost sorry to leave it last April for this grander place with all its splendor.

There was no wedding at all; that is, there were no invited guests, but sure, never had bride greater honor at her bridal than our Daisy had, for the church where the ceremony was performed, at a very early hour in the morning, was literally crowded with the halt, the lame, the maimed, and the blind; the slums of New York, gathered from every back street and by-lane and gutter; Daisy's "people," as she calls them, who came to see her married, and who, strangest of all, brought with them a present for the bride, a beautiful family Bible, golden-clasped and bound, and costing fifty dollars. Sandy McGraw presented it, and had written upon the fly leaf: "To the dearest friend we ever had we give this book as a slight token of how much we love her." Then followed upon a sheet of paper the names of the donors and how much each gave. Oh, how Daisy cried when she saw the ten cents and the five cents and the three cents and the one cent, and knew how it had all been earned and saved at some sacrifice for her. I do believe she would have kissed every one of them if Guy had permitted it. She did kiss the children and shook every hard, soiled hand there, and then Guy took her away and brought her to our home, where she has been ever since, the sweetest, merriest, happiest little creature that ever a man called wife, or a woman sister. She does leave her things round a little, to be sure, and she is not always ready for breakfast. I guess she never will wholly overcome those habits, but I can put up with them now better than I used to. Love makes a vast difference in our estimate of others, and she could scarcely ruffle me now, even if she kept breakfast

Mary J. Holmes

waiting every morning, and left her clothes lying three garments deep upon the floor. As for Guy—but his happiness is something I cannot describe. Nothing can disturb his peace, which is as firm as the everlasting hills. He does not caress her as much as he did once, but his thoughtful care of her is wonderful, and she is never long from his sight without his going to seek her.

God bless them both and keep them ever as they are now, at peace with Him and all in all to each other.

THE END

Choose from Thousands of 1stWorldLibrary Classics By

A. M. Barnard
Ada Leverson
Adolphus William Ward
Aesop
Agatha Christie
Alexander Aaronsohn
Alexander Kielland
Alexandre Dumas
Alfred Gatty
Alfred Ollivant
Alice Duer Miller
Alice Turner Curtis
Alice Dunbar
Allen Chapman
Alleyne Ireland
Ambrose Bierce
Amelia E. Barr
Amory H. Bradford
Andrew Lang
Andrew McFarland Davis
Andy Adams
Angela Brazil
Anna Alice Chapin
Anna Sewell
Annie Besant
Annie Hamilton Donnell
Annie Payson Call
Annie Roe Carr
Annonaymous
Anton Chekhov
Archibald Lee Fletcher
Arnold Bennett
Arthur C. Benson
Arthur Conan Doyle
Arthur M. Winfield
Arthur Ransome
Arthur Schnitzler
Arthur Train
Atticus
B.H. Baden-Powell
B. M. Bower
B. C. Chatterjee
Baroness Emmuska Orczy
Baroness Orczy
Basil King
Bayard Taylor
Ben Macomber
Bertha Muzzy Bower
Bjornstjerne Bjornson

Booth Tarkington
Boyd Cable
Bram Stoker
C. Collodi
C. E. Orr
C. M. Ingleby
Carolyn Wells
Catherine Parr Traill
Charles A. Eastman
Charles Amory Beach
Charles Dickens
Charles Dudley Warner
Charles Farrar Browne
Charles Ives
Charles Kingsley
Charles Klein
Charles Hanson Towne
Charles Lathrop Pack
Charles Romyn Dake
Charles Whibley
Charles Willing Beale
Charlotte M. Braeme
Charlotte M. Yonge
Charlotte Perkins Stetson
Clair W. Hayes
Clarence Day Jr.
Clarence E. Mulford
Clemence Housman
Confucius
Coningsby Dawson
Cornelis DeWitt Wilcox
Cyril Burleigh
D. H. Lawrence
Daniel Defoe
David Garnett
Dinah Craik
Don Carlos Janes
Donald Keyhoe
Dorothy Kilner
Dougan Clark
Douglas Fairbanks
E. Nesbit
E. P. Roe
E. Phillips Oppenheim
E. S. Brooks
Earl Barnes
Edgar Rice Burroughs
Edith Van Dyne
Edith Wharton

Edward Everett Hale
Edward J. O'Biren
Edward S. Ellis
Edwin L. Arnold
Eleanor Atkins
Eleanor Hallowell Abbott
Eliot Gregory
Elizabeth Gaskell
Elizabeth McCracken
Elizabeth Von Arnim
Ellem Key
Emerson Hough
Emilie F. Carlen
Emily Bronte
Emily Dickinson
Enid Bagnold
Enilor Macartney Lane
Erasmus W. Jones
Ernie Howard Pie
Ethel May Dell
Ethel Turner
Ethel Watts Mumford
Eugene Sue
Eugenie Foa
Eugene Wood
Eustace Hale Ball
Evelyn Everett-green
Everard Cotes
F. H. Cheley
F. J. Cross
F. Marion Crawford
Fannie E. Newberry
Federick Austin Ogg
Ferdinand Ossendowski
Fergus Hume
Florence A. Kilpatrick
Fremont B. Deering
Francis Bacon
Francis Darwin
Frances Hodgson Burnett
Frances Parkinson Keyes
Frank Gee Patchin
Frank Harris
Frank Jewett Mather
Frank L. Packard
Frank V. Webster
Frederic Stewart Isham
Frederick Trevor Hill
Frederick Winslow Taylor

Friedrich Kerst
Friedrich Nietzsche
Fyodor Dostoyevsky
G.A. Henty
G.K. Chesterton
Gabrielle E. Jackson
Garrett P. Serviss
Gaston Leroux
George A. Warren
George Ade
Geroge Bernard Shaw
George Cary Eggleston
George Durston
George Ebers
George Eliot
George Gissing
George MacDonald
George Meredith
George Orwell
George Sylvester Viereck
George Tucker
George W. Cable
George Wharton James
Gertrude Atherton
Gordon Casserly
Grace E. King
Grace Gallatin
Grace Greenwood
Grant Allen
Guillermo A. Sherwell
Gulielma Zollinger
Gustav Flaubert
H. A. Cody
H. B. Irving
H.C. Bailey
H. G. Wells
H. H. Munro
H. Irving Hancock
H. R. Naylor
H. Rider Haggard
H. W. C. Davis
Haldeman Julius
Hall Caine
Hamilton Wright Mabie
Hans Christian Andersen
Harold Avery
Harold McGrath
Harriet Beecher Stowe
Harry Castlemon
Harry Coghill
Harry Houidini

Hayden Carruth
Helent Hunt Jackson
Helen Nicolay
Hendrik Conscience
Hendy David Thoreau
Henri Barbusse
Henrik Ibsen
Henry Adams
Henry Ford
Henry Frost
Henry James
Henry Jones Ford
Henry Seton Merriman
Henry W Longfellow
Herbert A. Giles
Herbert Carter
Herbert N. Casson
Herman Hesse
Hildegard G. Frey
Homer
Honore De Balzac
Horace B. Day
Horace Walpole
Horatio Alger Jr.
Howard Pyle
Howard R. Garis
Hugh Lofting
Hugh Walpole
Humphry Ward
Ian Maclaren
Inez Haynes Gillmore
Irving Bacheller
Isabel Cecilia Williams
Isabel Hornibrook
Israel Abrahams
Ivan Turgenev
J.G.Austin
J. Henri Fabre
J. M. Barrie
J. M. Walsh
J. Macdonald Oxley
J. R. Miller
J. S. Fletcher
J. S. Knowles
J. Storer Clouston
J. W. Duffield
Jack London
Jacob Abbott
James Allen
James Andrews
James Baldwin

James Branch Cabell
James DeMille
James Joyce
James Lane Allen
James Lane Allen
James Oliver Curwood
James Oppenheim
James Otis
James R. Driscoll
Jane Abbott
Jane Austen
Jane L. Stewart
Janet Aldridge
Jens Peter Jacobsen
Jerome K. Jerome
Jessie Graham Flower
John Buchan
John Burroughs
John Cournos
John F. Kennedy
John Gay
John Glasworthy
John Habberton
John Joy Bell
John Kendrick Bangs
John Milton
John Philip Sousa
John Taintor Foote
Jonas Lauritz Idemil Lie
Jonathan Swift
Joseph A. Altsheler
Joseph Carey
Joseph Conrad
Joseph E. Badger Jr
Joseph Hergesheimer
Joseph Jacobs
Jules Vernes
Julian Hawthrone
Julie A Lippmann
Justin Huntly McCarthy
Kakuzo Okakura
Karle Wilson Baker
Kate Chopin
Kenneth Grahame
Kenneth McGaffey
Kate Langley Bosher
Kate Langley Bosher
Katherine Cecil Thurston
Katherine Stokes
L. A. Abbot
L. T. Meade

L. Frank Baum
Latta Griswold
Laura Dent Crane
Laura Lee Hope
Laurence Housman
Lawrence Beasley
Leo Tolstoy
Leonid Andreyev
Lewis Carroll
Lewis Sperry Chafer
Lilian Bell
Lloyd Osbourne
Louis Hughes
Louis Joseph Vance
Louis Tracy
Louisa May Alcott
Lucy Fitch Perkins
Lucy Maud Montgomery
Luther Benson
Lydia Miller Middleton
Lyndon Orr
M. Corvus
M. H. Adams
Margaret E. Sangster
Margret Howth
Margaret Vandercook
Margaret W. Hungerford
Margret Penrose
Maria Edgeworth
Maria Thompson Daviess
Mariano Azuela
Marion Polk Angellotti
Mark Overton
Mark Twain
Mary Austin
Mary Catherine Crowley
Mary Cole
Mary Hastings Bradley
Mary Roberts Rinehart
Mary Rowlandson
M. Wollstonecraft Shelley
Maud Lindsay
Max Beerbohm
Myra Kelly
Nathaniel Hawthrone
Nicolo Machiavelli
O. F. Walton
Oscar Wilde

Owen Johnson
P.G. Wodehouse
Paul and Mabel Thorne
Paul G. Tomlinson
Paul Severing
Percy Brebner
Percy Keese Fitzhugh
Peter B. Kyne
Plato
Quincy Allen
R. Derby Holmes
R. L. Stevenson
R. S. Ball
Rabindranath Tagore
Rahul Alvares
Ralph Bonehill
Ralph Henry Barbour
Ralph Victor
Ralph Waldo Emmerson
Rene Descartes
Ray Cummings
Rex Beach
Rex E. Beach
Richard Harding Davis
Richard Jefferies
Richard Le Gallienne
Robert Barr
Robert Frost
Robert Gordon Anderson
Robert L. Drake
Robert Lansing
Robert Lynd
Robert Michael Ballantyne
Robert W. Chambers
Rosa Nouchette Carey
Rudyard Kipling
Saint Augustine
Samuel B. Allison
Samuel Hopkins Adams
Sarah Bernhardt
Sarah C. Hallowell
Selma Lagerlof
Sherwood Anderson
Sigmund Freud
Standish O'Grady
Stanley Weyman
Stella Benson
Stella M. Francis

Stephen Crane
Stewart Edward White
Stijn Streuvels
Swami Abhedananda
Swami Parmananda
T. S. Ackland
T. S. Arthur
The Princess Der Ling
Thomas A. Janvier
Thomas A Kempis
Thomas Anderton
Thomas Bailey Aldrich
Thomas Bulfinch
Thomas De Quincey
Thomas Dixon
Thomas H. Huxley
Thomas Hardy
Thomas More
Thornton W. Burgess
U. S. Grant
Upton Sinclair
Valentine Williams
Various Authors
Vaughan Kester
Victor Appleton
Victor G. Durham
Victoria Cross
Virginia Woolf
Wadsworth Camp
Walter Camp
Walter Scott
Washington Irving
Wilbur Lawton
Wilkie Collins
Willa Cather
Willard F. Baker
William Dean Howells
William le Queux
W. Makepeace Thackeray
William W. Walter
William Shakespeare
Winston Churchill
Yei Theodora Ozaki
Yogi Ramacharaka
Young E. Allison
Zane Grey

www.ingramcontent.com/pod-product-compliance
Lightning Source LLC
Chambersburg PA
CBHW031843170626
46807CB00004B/1605